FINDING
SUPERMAN

FINDING SUPERMAN

Debating the Future of Public Education in America

TOURO COLLEGE LIBRARY
Kings Hwy

EDITED BY

Watson Scott Swail

Teachers College, Columbia University
New York and London

KH

Published by Teachers College Press, 1234 Amsterdam Avenue, New York, NY 10027

Library of Congress Cataloging-in-Publication Data

Finding Superman : debating the future of public education in America / edited by Watson Scott Swail.
    p. cm.
Includes index.
ISBN 978-0-8077-5330-9 (pbk.)—ISBN 978-0-8077-5331-6 (hardcover)
1. Public schools—United States. 2. Superman (Fictitious character) I. Swail, Watson Scott.
LA217.2.F53 2012
370.973—dc23

2011051100

ISBN 978-0-8077-5330-9 (paperback)
ISBN 978-0-8077-5331-6 (hardcover)

Printed on acid-free paper
Manufactured in the United States of America

19 18 17 16 15 14 13 12   8 7 6 5 4 3 2 1

6/25/13

For my parents, Gordon and Florence, who helped me understand that hard work opens the doors of opportunity. It is my hope that this book, and other efforts, will help open those doors for others who may not have won the parental lottery like I did.

CONTENTS

Preface

In 2010, Academy Award–winning writer and director Davis Guggenheim released *Waiting for "Superman,"* a documentary about educational inequity in America. The movie depicts five families and their parallel quest for a quality education and greater opportunities for their children.

Since the release of the movie, a mini-industry has spawned in its shadow, complete with a nonprofit organization, a website, a book, discussion guides, and grassroots efforts to "fix" education in this nation. Big names, including Bill Gates, Geoffrey Canada, and Michelle Rhee, have helped boost the relevance and influence of the documentary.

Proponents of *Waiting for "Superman"* point to the need to reform education and provide greater choice for parents: choice through the use of charter schools. Critics say the movie unfairly depicts the charter school movement as a panacea of educational opportunity and excellence. The truth lies somewhere in the middle: We are in great need of continued reform of public and private K–12 schooling in America, but charter schools, in isolation, most certainly will not solve all our educational inequities.

Guggenheim's *Waiting for "Superman"* provides a unique opportunity to take an inward look at not only the challenges of our education system, but the potential remedies to improve the conditions resulting from poverty and related social problems. The purpose of this book is not to attack Guggenheim's work. I, for one, believe he has done a great service to education and has helped focus viewers on issues that matter. While I disagree with some of the tenets of the movie, such as its overpowering suggestion that charter schools are the answer to our education reform questions, the movie provides a vivid portrayal of what the future looks like for too many of our children, left not only to the roll of a lottery ball, but to a larger social lottery of who is born to either advantage or disadvantage. As my colleague and friend Tom Mortenson says, the challenge with poor children is they can't choose their parents.

Waiting for "Superman" has the potential to serve as a foundation for an important dialogue regarding public education in America: a dialogue that too often becomes a shouting match of ideology—of left or right, blue or red—while ignoring the fact that children are damaged by our inability to do more about the educational and economic inequities that exist in every city, district, and state. Our focus should be on how we can eliminate the barriers to high-level education so that everyone, not just our entitled citizens, can benefit from what society has to offer.

While the movie was created to help bring focus to a real issue of equity and education, this book is designed to provide more depth and perspective on the issues presented in *Waiting for "Superman."* At best, the movie provides 90 minutes of entertainment and information. Geoffrey Canada is a compelling lead actor who extolls the need for education reform, but his work raises an important policy question: Is the Harlem Children's Zone scalable across the nation? Can others do what he has remarkably been able to accomplish? Michelle Rhee, former chancellor of the District of Columbia Public Schools, served as a lightning rod in both the movie and in public. Her hard-nosed techniques made above-the-fold news around the nation and catapulted her to stardom in the education reform arena after only a brief year and a half as a public school superintendent. Is she a saint or a pariah in the world of public education? Did she move the needle of school reform forward or pull it back? Of course, the children depicted in the movie provide the most compelling scenes, and while we feel for the girls and boys showcased in the closing scenes of the movie, we are left with emptiness and despair concerning what can be done to ameliorate these issues.

It is important to have ongoing and constructive dialogues about education reform; it is equally important that we capitalize on the attention created by the movie. However, it is critical that we ground the information and messages presented in *Waiting for "Superman"* in facts. The movie's rhetoric on charter schools and the fabulous graphics may be entertaining, but we can move forward only with a more concise, authentic dialogue about education reform. We cannot focus merely on the carefully crafted vignettes designed to tell a thoughtful story while also moving a clearly articulated agenda.

At the risk of grandstanding, what is at stake here is nothing less than the future of American society. Only through education will we retain our role in the world as influential partner, protector, and peacemaker. Only through education will we ensure that our way of life—our rights and freedoms—will be transferred to future generations. The importance of education and equity in this nation must not be understated: It is the foundation of almost everything we value as a society. It is critically important that we move forcefully toward improving the educational opportunity for all students, especially those that we have neglected, consciously or not, in our relatively brief history as a nation. That, in turn, will create exceptional advantages in our ability to compete globally while securing our way of life. The American Dream will survive only if we subscribe to Thomas Jefferson's tenet that a democracy requires an educated citizenry: "If a nation expects to be ignorant and free it expects what never was and never will be."[1] Ultimately, education is freedom.

Finding Superman provides an alternative lens to the messaging presented in *Waiting for "Superman."* To do so, we have brought together a diverse group of educators, researchers, and policymakers who were invited to participate in this book because they have distinct perspectives on both the movie and education at large. Through the following chapters, the authors provide details and information on the perspectives showcased in the movie. Some authors disagree vehemently with Guggenheim's portrayal of the public school system and take time to point out inaccuracies or misperceptions. Others use the movie as a launch pad for a deeper conversation about what we need to do to improve education in America, and perhaps beyond. This book is deliberately broad in its scope. I invited each author to share his or her impressions of *Waiting for "Superman"* and lead us into a dialogue about what this means for public education and school reform.

Readers are encouraged to use this book to consider, or perhaps reconsider, their thoughts and stance on public education and educational equity. This book, much like the movie that sparked the essays contained herein, provides much fodder for schools of education and public policy to discuss the politics of education and the processes involved in school reform. For policymakers, this book should start a new conversation—one based less on rhetoric and more on fact— about the role of government at each level of the system and how we make positive educational change. For parents, teachers, and other stakeholders of public education, this book should be, at a minimum, a clear reminder that not all seems as it necessarily is and that school reform is complex and challenging. We have a responsibility to look at varied points of view and interest and not accept as fact things that aren't necessarily representative of reality.

I hope this book provides additional insights and perspectives on teaching and learning in America. *Waiting for "Superman"* gives us a great opportunity to engage the issues of school reform, school choice, and high-level education for all. But only if we take these opportunities and use them wisely.

—Watson Scott Swail, EdD, June 2012

NOTE

1. Retrieved from http://en.wikipedia.org/wiki/Thomas_Jefferson.

CHAPTER 1

Finding Superman

Watson Scott Swail

Davis Guggenheim's *Waiting for "Superman"* allows us to put a mirror to our education system and take a long look at how we serve all students, not just those from more advantaged families. While several chapters in this book fact check claims made in the movie, it is also important to use this opportunity to consider areas where we can improve public education rather than focus on ideological disagreements, such as the discourse of charter schools and voucher programs.

Focusing on the positive is difficult. We live in a nation that is free-market in nature and capitalist by design. And while these things have made us one of the great nations of the world, they also ensure inequities in our economy and social systems. Capitalism makes for a tough reality for many people. By its premise, capitalism evokes a Darwinian spirit in us; it *is* survival of the fittest. America has always risen to the challenge through the challenge itself. We are an "us or them" nation, and we like to be number one.

For this reason, it is interesting, albeit disappointing, that we have chosen not to be number one in the education, health, and welfare of our citizens. I use "chosen" with purpose: Our policies, perspectives, and certainly our politics on these issues are conscious choices about our priorities and expectations of one another. America puts a large emphasis on personal responsibility, which, in itself, is not a bad thing. But the ramifications of this philosophy continue to play out in welfare, minimum wage, health, and most certainly education policy, to the detriment of many of our citizens who reside on the lower rungs of the economic ladder.

I lump these issues together because a discussion about education and equity is not solely about public education. It is not simply about school choice, or vouchers, or charter schools. It is about the "health and welfare" of our youth, which have a direct and correlated relationship with our ability, as a nation, to remain globally competitive. This is about commerce. And that, above all, is truly Darwinian.

Many of the chapters in this book touch on the Finnish experience, which takes education as an essential part of the social service system of the country. Education works in Finland because the social safety nets are solidly in place. Finns have fewer worries about health care, unemployment, and welfare than U.S. residents do because the state puts these programs in place and does not leave individuals to fend for themselves. The Finnish social safety net allows the education system not only to work, but to work tremendously well. True, Finland is not nearly as diverse a nation as the United States, but there are many lessons we can learn from Finnish policies and practices.

The U.S. education system has become an easy target for critics. The Program in International Student Assessment (PISA) and other international surveys clearly show the United States at or below average on comparative data. But the data do not tell a full and complete story, either. The difference in these comparisons is the size and scope of the issues. It is important to consider that there are over 55 million K–12 students in in the United States, approximately 90% of whom are enrolled in public schools.[1] This education is distributed through 50-plus state governments and territories that enjoy local control of education. Taken at a glance, it is a mindboggling issue to get our collective heads around: How do we educate, with equity and quality, 55 million students? How do we make them all "college ready," since that is the current national focus in education in order to retain our international dominance in business and industry? How do we ensure that our system is not, as *Waiting for "Superman"* suggests, a conveyer belt that tracks "good," more advantaged students to college and other students to something definitively lesser? With such a humongous system of education, it has been easy for us to fall into the conveyer mindset: 55 million students. How do we possibly educate that many students well? The answer, as the movie suggests, is to provide rich learning environments for all students.

Education in America is complex, given the devolution of our political system. Education is tied to state governance, regulation, and responsibility, and applied to local education agencies (education speak for "districts"), with oversight from a federal Department of Education.[2] Add in teacher unions, colleges of education, national associations, and influential philanthropic organizations, and some might think that it is amazing we do as well as we do. But *Waiting for "Superman"* is absolutely correct in one important area: we need to be better.

Capitalism is alive and well within our education system. Through the service of millions of students and teachers, and through the diversity of the system described above, the reality is that some students, some classrooms, and some school districts provide a level of education that stands at the top of international rankings. Conversely, other districts and schools are provided with fewer resources, resulting in lesser outcomes for students. The truth is clear: Not all states are created equal in the United States of America. Some states redistribute funding in an equitable way in an attempt to ameliorate issues of wealth and poverty. Within school districts, some schools, often due to wealth diversity within the district, are better off than others. And we know, as do teachers, administrators, and policymakers, that some classrooms are better than others. Our system is uniquely diverse, to the benefit of some and the detriment of others.

Still, I support the argument that the United States does a relatively good job of educating the masses. The problem is that we don't do a good enough job of serving all students, especially those who (a) are from low-income backgrounds, (b) have no family college history (i.e., first-generation), (c) are ESL (English Second Language), and (d) have special education needs.

In *Waiting for "Superman,"* Harlem Children Zone CEO Geoffrey Canada has it right: "Almost everybody who comes in to do school, they come in and try and save kids after they are lost." For a large group of youngsters in America, the game is lost before it has even started. Over the past two decades, we have learned much about brain chemistry and the importance of early childhood learning, especially with regard to development before the age of five. Regardless, over 75% of our 4-year-olds do not have access to state-funded prekindergarten.3 Findings from the National Assessment of Educational Progress (NAEP) show that, while fourth- and eighth-grade math and reading scores have trended north since 1990, the gap in scores between White and Asian students on the one hand and Black and Hispanic students on the other, strongly evident in fourth grade, remains in eighth grade.[4] Once students finish 8th grade, the game is essentially over. We can't effectively remediate that much poor education.

Equity and excellence are difficult to attain in any system, especially one as large and diverse as in the United States. International comparisons can be useful but should not serve as our primary measuring stick. A better measure is our internal assessment of how we educate all students, regardless of background. Mahatma Ghandi famously stated that, "A nation's greatness is measured by how it treats its weakest members." This should be the guiding principle for American education, if not American government.

The task of making our schools better for all students is not for the faint of heart. As we know, it is terribly difficult, complex, and even controversial work. Over the past five decades, much research and effort, not to mention funding, has been expended to improve our education system. It would be disingenuous to suggest that we aren't better in many ways. We are. Still, we know we can do much better. Our top students are as good as any students in the world—perhaps better. But we fail to meet the same goals and high expectations for those outside this upper echelon of academic achievement.

The list of things to improve is seemingly endless. For this chapter, I wish to focus on three specific areas regarding how we improve teachers, schools, and learning in order to achieve greater equity and opportunity for all students.

BETTER TEACHERS

"But the one thing those who work in the trenches know, is you can't have a great school without great teachers."
—Davis Guggenheim

A good school is predicated first and foremost on the quality of its teaching staff. While it takes a village to raise a child, it most certainly takes good teachers to help students learn.

There are 3.6 million teachers in America's public schools.[5] Each one has earned a 4-year degree at an accredited college of education or possesses an equivalent certificate. Most of us can remember key teachers in our lives who helped pave the way to our success. Yet there is still a sense that our teachers are not good enough; that they are teachers only because they could not possibly do anything else. Remember the old adage: "Those who can't, teach. Those who can't teach, teach teachers." While mildly amusing (it is), it holds little truth. Walk into almost any school in the United States and you will find dedicated, well-trained teachers who care about their students. For 7 years, I was one of them.

But the reality is this: Even after completing a 4-year degree program, 9.2% of public school teachers and 21.1% of private school teachers under the age of 30 leave the teaching force each year,[6] the highest percentage of any age group outside the retirement population (i.e., age 60 and over). Additionally, it is reported that almost half of new teachers leave the profession within 5 years.[7] Some teachers leave because of other, sometimes more lucrative opportunities beyond education,[8] while others leave because they simply don't like teaching. It is probable that we both lose good teachers and retain bad teachers concurrently. The "Dance of the Lemons" offered in *Waiting for "Superman,"* where bad teachers are passed around from school to school, surely occurs. And while unions may have a hand in this, it is more an indictment of low expectations and bad school governance than anything else.

It is for all of these reasons that we need to retool teaching in America. It starts by furthering the professionalization of teaching.

That, of course, is an outcome of many activities over a long period of time. Professionalism and respect occur, over time, through accountability and excellence. Teaching is on that pathway but needs to push forward.

So it begins with how we attract, prepare, and retain teachers. People come to teaching for a variety of reasons. While salary isn't a primary reason that people leave the profession, it may be a reason that people do not enter it. A 2009 poll by the Hoover Foundation found that the public dramatically underestimated the average salary of teachers, guessing $33,000 instead of the $47,000 average across all states.[9] Still, with a starting teaching salary of approximately $31,500,[10] it is possible that many potentially great teacher candidates choose other careers before teaching. The National Center on Education and the Economy, in the 2006 report *Tough Times,* encouraged the recruitment of teachers from the top third of high school graduates, using starting and continuing salaries as a motivator to go into teaching. *Tough Times* suggests paying beginning teachers $45,000, up to $95,000 for "typical" teachers, and as much as $110,000 for top teachers.[11]

To be fair, attracting highly-qualified individuals into teaching isn't the only concern. Giving them proven tools to succeed is also critical. Unfortunately, Arthur Levine, in his 2006 study of U.S. colleges of education, found that most colleges don't do a very good job of preparing future teachers. In his own words, Levine says that as many as two thirds of our teachers are enrolled in programs that have "inadequate curriculums, low standards, and faculty disconnected from the schools."[12] Similar to the diversity in our schools, there is diversity in our colleges of education. Some are good and some are simply mediocre. We can increase the efficacy of colleges of education by bringing standards of expectations and practices to the teaching profession and higher education system. Levine suggests we focus on stringent quality control in our colleges of education, with deep content knowledge and an understanding of how teachers teach and how students learn. While colleges of education should be on the front lines of educational research and reform and ahead of the pedagogical curve, they aren't, and much of that is due to the lack of quality and foresight of university faculty. I strongly subscribe to the Professional Practice School concept of the 1980s and 1990s, where colleges of education work in tandem with school districts, placing faculty within schools rather than at arm's length. The premise of teaching should be like that of medicine and law: professionals "practicing." Teachers should be researchers, and faculty should be teachers. Only through the close interaction of the two can we truly have cutting-edge teaching and learning, led by what happens in the classroom and with a mindset of improvement and empiricism.

What school districts do with new teachers has much to do with the quality of teaching and learning. Teacher induction programs—those that provide initial support and professional development to new teachers—are critical to future success, and, in many cases, future retention. Recent studies are equivocal on the impact on retention, practice, and student outcomes of induction programs,[13] but what school districts do with new teachers is surely important to their immediate impact in the classroom.

It is difficult to talk about teacher efficacy without talking about teacher assessment. In *Waiting for "Superman,"* Stanford professor Eric Hanushek says that if we could eliminate the bottom-performing 6–10% of teachers—the "bad" teachers—and replace them with even average teachers, student performance would exceed that of Finland. Hanushek's analysis isn't foolproof, of course, because his determination of good versus bad is predicated primarily on standardized test scores, and we understand, as in the assessment of student outcomes, that standardized test scores are but one measure of proficiency and that others, such as performance reviews, are also crucial in determining teacher efficacy. *Waiting for "Superman"'s* Davis Guggenheim says that the teacher evaluation process "seems like a strange game to me." It may be, but assessment is a difficult process. If not for that strange game, then what? No one wants burdensome complexity, but we also don't want the process to be based solely on limited information from one test or even one observation. Performance reviews need to be appropriate and fair for all. Unlike the Finnish system, which has limited supervision of teachers and no formal evaluation, our teachers should be thoroughly evaluated and assessed for what they do well and where they need continued professional development. This is part of the "practice" of teaching and shouldn't be anything that we recoil from. Rather, we must be mindful of the implications and resources required to improve the quality of teachers in our system.

Complicating the process is the potential use of these evaluations for merit-pay purposes. Proponents of merit pay suggest this will make the teaching force better. Considering, however, that there is no single measure that can determine who or what is "best," using the same process to determine who should be paid more—or less—seems challenging. To the chagrin of these proponents, teaching is essentially a sociopolitical system. Suggesting that we have variations in teacher pay tied to student outcomes seems egregious in many ways (see Chapter 9 by Ben Levin for a richer discussion on this issue). Harvard professor Richard Murnane and Michigan's David Cohen note that, with regard to merit pay, there are no clearly defined behaviors that clearly result in high performance among teachers.[14] In fact, they suggest that teachers can do many things to impress principals or assessors that have little to do with teacher efficacy.

If we truly want to look at merit systems for teachers, we must be very mindful about what measures we use to address the issue.

BETTER SCHOOLS

The schools where we send our children matter. The physical condition of the school, the technology, even the type of school and community matter greatly in the education "value added" for students. *Waiting for "Superman"* did not depict horrific schools, but they do exist, and many studies are able to quantify the impact of aged buildings on learning.[15] Pulitzer-prize winning author Ron Suskind, in his award-winning book *A Hope in the Unseen*, documents the challenges associated with growing up and learning in a low-income, dilapidated community in Washington, DC.[16] A 2008 report conducted for the American Federation of Teachers estimated a $254 billion shortfall in school infrastructure funding in the United States.[17] There are schools that many of us would not want our own children attending and there are teachers who refuse to work in these places.

It is well noted that not all schools are created equal, even within a single public school district. Schools are a product of the real estate that surrounds them. Affluent areas typically have nicer schools than poorer neighborhoods, and many of us purchase houses according to SAT/ACT score: the higher the test score, the more expensive the housing, with income being the socioeconomic filter. Of course, the converse is probably more causal. Not only do more-affluent parents provide more educational support to their children, on average, than low-income families, but they provide additional fiscal resources to their local public school that aren't available in other, less-affluent areas.

The financial resources of a school and a school district impact the availability and use of technology to support learning. The availability of laptops, smart boards, and even basic Internet impacts the pedagogical approaches used in a school. Regardless of whether one believes that technology impacts learning, the absence of technology distances education from the world at large.

Our prior discussion about better teachers is impacted by the availability of appropriate tools for learning. Currently, I serve as the principal investigator of a new magnet school in a large, urban school district, where every student receives a laptop computer. At this time we have not established a direct linkage between the laptop and student learning, but we clearly see how teaching has been improved in this school compared with other schools. The technology definitely has increased cooperation among teachers and increased connectivity with their students. The use of wikis and other online technologies, in tandem with smart boards, certainly has elevated teaching when teachers are well trained and lesson plans and pedagogy are designed appropriately.

Building better schools ultimately requires better leadership. We previously spoke about teachers, but good teachers are supported by great administrators and staff. In my research studies, I have found that buildings with administrators who posessed a data-driven and outcome-focused outlook, complemented by a firm understanding of organizational management, were in much better shape than those with leaders who did not possess these attributes. As with teachers, appropriate professional development and assessment is in order. And as with teachers, we must be mindful of using solely student outcomes to measure the quality of professional practice.

As a case in point, *Waiting for "Superman"* depicts the challenges faced by Michelle Rhee, then-Chancellor of the Washington, DC public schools. The District of Columbia has had a long history of difficulties, and it needed yet another person to try to shake up the system. Others have certainly tried and failed, so 39-year-old Rhee was brought in to do the job. Unfortunately, she came in with a conflict-based leadership style and made enemies from day one.[18] Her job was very difficult, certainly, but it is arguable whether she possessed the leadership skills to pull off this massive undertaking. One simply can't take a divisive tack and expect to reach shared goals. By the time the movie was released, Rhee was long gone from the District of Columbia.

Organizational change, well beyond that of education, requires a firm understanding of how people work, think, and engage. We gain momentum not by shutting people out, but by bringing them in. We work hard to get people on our wagon, and not by firing our way out of the corral.[19] Leadership is having a clear vision of what you want to do and the astuteness to understand what it takes to make that vision a reality. In translation? Possession of a firm knowledge of the issues partnered with the political acumen to navigate the process. It means understanding that we may not get everything we want, but we push forward in a meaningful manner. Education is an incremental notion; you can't clear the board and start over. Charter schools think they can do this, and they fail more often than they succeed because there is no such thing as a blank slate. You cannot erase the previous training of teachers and administrators, even in charter schools. Nor can one erase the histories and realities of children and families in their community. But you can begin to change perceptions and expectations—and at some point conditions—through carefully articulated conversations and policies aimed at increasing achievement and focusing on students.

Many critics, including those in this book, suggest that *Waiting for "Superman"* is an advertisement for charter schools and school choice. Given the schools presented in the movie—one of which I serve as lead evaluator for—this is an easy conclusion to draw. In the opening minutes of the movie, Davis Guggenheim comments that he is lucky because he has "a choice." Diane Ravitch, in Chapter 2, makes note that Guggenheim attended the exclusive (and expensive) Sidwell Friends School (a.k.a., Chelsea's, Malia's, and Sasha's school) in Washington, DC. But Guggenheim is right: He has a choice. And those who have a choice make it. We make it by sending our children to private schools or by purchasing more expensive housing in better neighborhoods because we know those schools are better.

But charters for charters' sake aren't necessarily better than public schools, as other contributors to this book have noted. The well-cited CREDO study, referenced in several chapters in this book, showcases what many of us have known for the past decade: charter schools are as volatile with regard to student outcomes as public schools. And as the CREDO study illustrates, many charter schools do worse than public schools and only a handful (17%) do better. I have seen firsthand the good and the bad of charter schools. In fact, I have been involved in and led evaluations of both Knowledge Is Power Program (KIPP) schools and the DC-based SEED schools. These schools are at the top of the charter lists and part of the "17%." Even so, administrators and teachers at both schools will tell you that teaching is challenging, and teaching students from low-income backgrounds can be a larger challenge due to the many forces that students (and families) must endure in order to learn. But the bad charters—the 37% that perform worse than their public peers—arguably do a large disservice to students and families, leaving them essentially high and dry.

The reporting in the movie (and the message it implies) is unfortunate, because it gives an improper impression of charter schools and public schools. When Bill Gates announces: "The top charter schools are sending 90 percent of their kids to four-year colleges," he essentially is saying that it is because they *are* charter schools. In truth, there are hundreds of public schools that send more than 90% of their students to college.[20] In fact, many send 98–100% of their students to college. This isn't a "charter" thing; it is a "good school" thing.

The movie makes a point that critics believe that successful charter schools cannot be brought to scale. In truth, scalability is a very difficult science. What Geoffrey Canada is doing in New York is remarkable, but it isn't replicable in a real way. Why? Because he is fortunate to have his fingers on big New York money. The Harlem Children's Zone (HCZ) has a reported trust fund of $200 million in private money that is invested in an offshore account. This is a big-dollar operation. And, to be fair, Canada's 2010 compensation of $450,872 and the VP for Development's $400,000 salary are not typical of any school district.[21] While I am all in favor of more HCZs, I also understand the limitations on their ability to be replicated and scaled up.

The KIPP schools are the only charter mechanism that has really been scaled up with any success. According to the KIPP website, there are currently 109 KIPP schools in 20 states, and they reportedly are doing well academically. I say "reportedly" because information and data on KIPP are kept fairly close to the vest and can be difficult to attain.[22] KIPP provides links to research studies on its website, including that of my own organization's (Educational Policy Institute) 2005 study, and even some of those studies acknowledge average gains in student outcomes.[23]

True efforts to build better schools must look at the community as a whole. If anything is to be learned from the Finnish experience, it is that the community and its related social safety nets matter. Finnish students do not worry about health care, about welfare, or about the cost of college. At a recent conference I attended in Toronto, convened jointly by Stanford University and the University of Toronto,[24] there was a general consensus among the PISA and other international data that social safety nets, such as health care and welfare, were a common thread in countries that academically outperform the United States.

Waiting for "Superman" makes the comment that "experts tend to blame failing schools on failing neighborhoods. But reformers have begun to believe the opposite—that the problem of failing neighborhoods might be blamed on failing schools." This, again, is unfortunate, because clearly the community builds the school. There is reciprocity, of course, but a school alone cannot be blamed for the direction a community takes, and a community must be fully responsible for what happens inside its schools.

The message is clear: Good schools require community buy-in. Rarely do schools excel when the local constituency is not involved. It can happen, but a good school can help a good community become great, and vice versa.

BETTER LEARNING

Perhaps the best quote in *Waiting for "Superman"* comes courtesy of *Newsweek*'s Jonathan Alter: "Nowadays, if you don't go to college, you're kinda screwed in America. And America's kinda screwed." There is a current push in the United States for more higher education. To be globally competitive, the saying goes, we need more people coming out of our high schools "college ready" and matriculating to 2- and 4-year institutions. This "higher education arms race" has been joined by two major foundations—Lumina Foundation for Education and the Bill & Melinda Gates Foundation—as well as the U.S. Department of Education. Unfortunately, the current discussion sometimes focused on how many graduates we need, rather than on how we get our youth ready for college-level studies at the end of high school.

In order to prepare our students for college, we not only need top-quality teachers in top-quality schools, but top-quality curriculum and pedagogy. The challenge, from a U.S. perspective, is in our geopolitical diversity. With each state legislating over its own education priorities, we have 50-plus systems of education working simultaneously toward similar goals for youth and adult learners. But the diversity of curriculum is seemingly even more vast. Michigan State's Bill Schmidt, who directed the Third International Mathematics and Science Study (TIMSS) for the U.S. National Research Center, once said that the challenge for the United States is our proclivity to keep adding to the curriculum without ever taking anything out, leaving us in an impossible situation of trying to teach more within the scope of limited time and materials. Schmidt also suggested that U.S. students do not perform well because their instruction is neither "coherent nor consistent."[25]

There has been recent movement for national standards for K–12 curriculum led by the National Governors Association and the Council of Chief State School Officers. The Common Core State Standards Initiative has developed K–12 standards to ensure that students, across all states and territories, will be prepared for college and career.[26] To date, the standards have been signed by 45 of the 50 states, plus the District of Columbia, the U.S. Virgin Islands, and the Northern Mariana Islands. While some critics see these as "federal standards," they have been developed in a grassroots, optional manner, completely free from federal influence. This is the first time in our nation's history that states are working jointly to ensure that curriculum is parallel across all states.

The common core standards have the potential to form a solid foundation from which we can provide equitable learning opportunities for all students. Important to this process ultimately will be the development of pedagogies to teach the standards along with parallel assessments that effectively measure teaching and learning. I argue that one of the reasons we have such large gaps in learning is because we do not have consistent standards of learning and standards of teaching. Curriculum and pedagogy are so variable across states that learning outcomes are somewhat meaningless because the content and the measures are so diverse. With an agreed-upon set of academic standards, we have a much better opportunity to determine who is learning and at what pace. Only then can we seriously start improving conditions in the United States.

The standards are only part of what we need to do to improve teaching and learning. Understanding that not all students learn at the same level and pace, we need to move away from our age-based K–12 system and toward a more diversified approach to learning. The advent of powerful technologies provides us with greater opportunity than at any time in our history to develop individual learning plans that are diversified for the uniqueness of each student. Many schools are now using distributed learning technologies to access AP and other college-level classes that they previously could not offer due to their size. Our ability to radically change how teaching and learning occur is now tangible. But we must do the work to facilitate the development of education modules and pedagogies that fully harness these technologies. Only then can we benefit from these advanced tools.

Alas, this is yet another area of learning where the haves and have nots live different realities, not just in terms of having the appropriate technology available in the schools, but of having teachers and aides who know how to use technology as a learning tool, in tandem with curriculum.

CONCLUSION

This chapter has provided a macro view of some of the elements necessary to push our public and private schools forward, further engaging our youth so that they can become not only college ready, but ready for a new global stage where high-level learning will be the common thread of success.

The challenges to moving forward are great. We must move away from the politics of divisiveness and work in a bipartisan manner to push the needs of our nation and our youth forward—not an easy thing to do, but necessary for our continued evolution. We must work toward a more seamless system of education so that students do not get lost between middle and high school, not to mention between high school and college. Students need clarity about how the different levels of education connect; they need to see the relevance in what they learn and how it relates not only to their world, but also to the broader world that is transformed by our diversity in culture, emerging technologies, and our struggling and increasingly-connected economies. Our students should never see education as merely a game or puzzle. It is our responsibility to help connect the dots so they can see the utility of education and understand the pathway for their future.

As Guggenheim states in *Waiting for "Superman,"* "Great schools won't come from Superman. They will come from you." He could not be more correct. "We" are Superman. There are no silver bullets, no quick fixes. There is no one person or agency that can ameliorate the barriers and conditions that plague our education system. As Geoffrey Canada says in *Waiting for "Superman,"* "We know we have the tools to save those kids. People are doing it every day now."

We need to create better teachers, better schools, and better learning opportunities for our students so that we can put the lotteries behind us—so that every child and every family can see the connections between school and work and envision a bright future through education.

NOTES

1. U.S. Department of Education, National Center for Education Statistics, *Digest of Education Statistics, 2010* (NCES 2011-015) (2011), Table 3, http://nces.ed.gov/fastfacts/display.asp?id=65.

2. The U.S. Department of Education is but one federal agency involved in public schools. The U.S. Department of Defense operates the largest school district in the world, educating American students at U.S. bases around the country and the world. The U.S. Department of Agriculture is influential in school lunches, and the Department of Health and Human Services is involved in the safety and well-being of students at all levels.

3. Pew Charitable Trusts, http://www.pewtrusts.org/our_work_detail.aspx?id=92.

4. U.S. Department of Education, *Findings in Brief: Reading and Mathematics 2011: National Assessment of Educational Progress at Grades 4 and 8* (Washington, DC: Institute of Education Sciences, National Center for Education Statistics, 2011).

5. Retrieved from http://nces.ed.gov/fastfacts/display.asp?id=28.

6. Retrieved from http://nces.ed.gov/programs/coe/indicator_tat.asp.

7. Retrieved from http://www.washingtonpost.com/wp-dyn/content/article/2006/05/08/AR2006050801344.html.

8. The primary reason young teachers leave teaching is for other career opportunities, and only 6.5% left for salary or benefits. For further information, see Benjamin Scafidi, David L. Sjoquist, and Todd R. Stinebrickner, "Do Teachers Really Leave for Higher Paying Jobs in Alternative Occupations?" *CIBC Working Paper Series*, 2005, http://economics.uwo.ca/centres/cibc/wp2005/Stinebrickner05.pdf.

9. See Paul Peterson's "What the Public Thinks of Public Schools," *Wall Street Journal*, September 8, 2009, http://online.wsj.com/article/SB10001424052970203440104574400850103134572.html.

10. Retrieved from http://www.teacherportal.com/teacher-salaries-by-state.

11. See p. 13, http://www.ncee.org/wp-content/uploads/2010/04/Executive-Summary.pdf.

12. Retrieved from http://www.boston.com/news/education/higher/articles/2006/10/31/a_higher_bar_for_future_teachers/.

13. Mathematica Policy Research conducted a study in 2010 for the U.S. Department of Education that found that induction programs had a null effect on these items (see http://ies.ed.gov/ncee/pubs/20104027/). However, other studies, such as Smith and Ingersoll, 2004, found quite large impacts from induction programs (see http://www.edu.haifa.ac.il/userfiles/file/lead_files_2/bibliography/Smith_%20Ingersoll_04.pdf).

14. R. J. Murnane and D. K. Cohen, *Merit Pay and the Evaluation Problem: Understanding Why Most Merit Pay Plans Fail and a Few Survive* (California Institute for Research on Educational Finance and Governance, Stanford University, 1985). (ERIC Document ED 270 842), http://www.eric.ed.gov/PDFS/ED270842.pdf.

15. K. Tanner and E. Jago, *The Influence of the School Facility on Student Achievement* (University of Georgia, 1999).

16. R. Suskind, *A Hope in the Unseen: An American Odyssey from the Inner City to the Ivy League* (New York: Broadway Books, 1999).

17. Retrieved from http://esciencenews.com/articles/2009/01/22/new.study.school.infrastructure.could.influence.obamas.economic.stimulus.plan.

18. According to the *Washington Post* (December 3, 2011), "Everyone wanted D.C. public schools to get better. But which schools and better for whom? Adrian Fenty won the mayoralty by promising he'd improve schools throughout the city, but while his dynamo of a schools chief, Michelle Rhee, blazed a trail of firings, hirings and renovations through every ward, she did so with a brazen disregard for local politics and the sensitivities of race and class. The result was dozens of shuttered schools, stunning new facilities at many D.C. schools, a new generation of teachers, a one-term mayor (whose replacement immediately showed Rhee the door) and a resurgence of black frustration over the city's changing racial and economic demographics." See http://www.washingtonpost.com/local/washington-post-magazines-25th-anniversary-25-moments-that-changed-washington-most-since-1986/2011/09/16/gIQACnZiHO_story.html.

19. However, I will be the first to suggest that firing can be a critical component of change when conducted strategically and fairly.

20. Retrieved from http://www.thedailybeast.com/newsweek/features/2011/americas-best-high-schools.html.

21. These figures are based on 2007 data; see http://www.forbes.com/lists/2008/14/charities08_Harlem-Childrens-Zone_CH0265.html. The 2010 Form 990 (the tax return for a tax-exempt organization) for Harlem Children's Zone shows $132 million in investment income and $43.4 million in real estate assets. See also http://www.theepochtimes.com/n2/united-states/harlem-childrens-zone-gets-91-million-54279-all.html and http://www.brookings.edu/reports.2010/0720_hcz_whitehurst.aspx

22. My organization, the Educational Policy Institute, conducted a data study for KIPP schools in 2005. While the findings were generally positive, we were not able to collect student-level data for the schools and were provided with only school-level

data rather than student unit-record data. While we had some belief that the data were clean and real, we are unable to certify the results.

23. For instance, a 2008 4-year outcome study of a KIPP school by University of Memphis researchers McDonald, Ross, Abney, and Zoblotsky found somewhat diminished results. "While the majority of the comparisons directionally favored KIPP students this year, only the 5th grade mathematics comparison was significant. The loss of the school principal and increased student behavior issues are interpreted as likely contributing factors." This statement suggests that KIPP schools have similar challenges, like leadership, to those that other public schools must navigate. See http://www.kipp.org/files/dmfile/CREP_KIPP_Diamond_Year4.pdf.

24. Achieving Equity Through Innovation: A Canada–United States Colloquium, October 27–28, 2010, Toronto, ON, http://edpolicy.stanford.edu/events/357.

25. A. Beatty, ed., *Results of the Third International Mathematics and Science Study* (Washington, DC: National Academies Press, 1997), 29, http://www.nap.edu/catalog.php?record_id=5937.

26. See http://www.corestandards.org/.

CHAPTER 2

The Myth of Charter Schools

Diane Ravitch

Ordinarily, documentaries about education attract little attention and seldom, if ever, reach neighborhood movie theaters. Davis Guggenheim's *Waiting for "Superman"* is different. It arrived in September 2010 with the biggest publicity splash I have ever seen for a documentary. Not only was it the subject of major stories in *Time* and *New York*, but it was featured twice on *The Oprah Winfrey Show* and was the centerpiece of several days of programming by NBC, including an interview with President Obama.

Two other films expounding the same arguments—*The Lottery* and *The Cartel*—were released between late 2009 and mid-2010, but they received far less attention than Guggenheim's film. His reputation as the director of the Academy Award–winning *An Inconvenient Truth*, about global warming, contributed to the anticipation surrounding *Waiting for "Superman,"* but the media frenzy suggested something more. Guggenheim presents the popularized version of an account of American public education that is promoted by some of the nation's most powerful figures and institutions.

The message of these films has become alarmingly familiar: American public education is a failed enterprise. The problem is not money. Public schools already spend too much. Test scores are low because there are so many bad teachers, whose jobs are protected by powerful unions. Students drop out because the schools fail them, but they could accomplish practically anything if they were saved from bad teachers. They would get higher test scores if schools could fire more bad teachers and pay more to good ones. The only hope for the future of our society, especially for poor Black and Hispanic children, is escape from public schools, especially to charter schools, which are funded mostly by the government but controlled by private organizations, many of them operating to make a profit.

The Cartel maintains that we must not only create more charter schools, but provide vouchers so that children can flee incompetent public schools and attend private schools. There, we are led to believe, teachers will be caring and highly skilled (unlike the lazy dullards in public schools); the schools will have high expectations and test scores will soar; and all children will succeed academically, regardless of their circumstances. *The Lottery* echoes the main story line of *Waiting for "Superman"*: It is about children who are desperate to avoid the New York City public schools and eager to win a spot in a shiny new charter school in Harlem.

For many people, these arguments require a willing suspension of disbelief. Most Americans graduated from public schools, and most went from school to college or the workplace without thinking that their school had limited their chances. There was a time—which now seems distant—when most people assumed that students' performance in school was determined largely by their own efforts and by the circumstances and support of their family, not by their teachers. There were good teachers and mediocre teachers, even bad teachers; but in the end, most public schools offered ample opportunity for education to those willing to pursue it. The annual Gallup Poll about education shows that Americans are overwhelmingly dissatisfied with the quality of the nation's schools, but 77% of public school parents award their own child's public school a grade of A or B, the highest level of approval since the question first was asked in 1985.

Waiting for "Superman" and the other films appeal to a broad apprehension that the nation is falling behind in global competition. If the economy is a shambles, if poverty persists for significant segments of the population, if American kids are not as serious about their studies as their peers in other nations, the schools must be to blame. At last we have the culprit on which we can pin our anger, our palpable sense that something is very wrong with our society, that we are on the wrong track, and that America is losing the race for global dominance. It is not globalization or deindustrialization or poverty or our coarse popular culture or predatory financial practices that bear responsibility: It's the public schools, their teachers, and their unions.

The inspiration for *Waiting for "Superman"* began, Guggenheim explains, as he drove his own children to a private school, past the neighborhood schools with low test scores. He wondered about the fate of the children whose families did not have the choice of schools available to his own children. What was the quality of their education? He was sure it must be terrible. The press release for the film says that he wondered, "How heartsick and worried did *their* parents feel as they dropped their kids off this morning?" Guggenheim is a graduate of Sidwell Friends, the elite private school in Washington, DC, where President Obama's daughters are enrolled. The public schools that he passed by each morning must have seemed as hopeless and dreadful to him as the public schools in Washington that his own parents had shunned.

Waiting for "Superman" tells the story of five children who enter a lottery to win a coveted place in a charter school. Four of them seek to escape the public schools; one was asked to leave a Catholic school because her mother couldn't afford the tuition. Four of the children are Black or Hispanic and live in gritty neighborhoods, while the one White child lives in a leafy suburb. We come to know each of these children and their families; we learn about their dreams for the future; we see that they are lovable; and we identify with them. By the end of the film, we are rooting for them as the day of the lottery approaches.

In each of the schools to which they have applied, the odds against them are large. Anthony, a fifth grader in Washington, DC, applies to the SEED charter boarding school, where there are 61 applicants for 24 places. Francisco is a first-grade student in the Bronx whose mother (a social worker with a graduate degree) is desperate to get him out of the New York City public schools and into a charter school; she applies to a Harlem Success Academy school where he is one of 792 applicants for 40 places. Bianca is the kindergarten student in Harlem whose mother cannot afford Catholic school tuition; she enters the lottery at another Harlem Success Academy school, as one of 767 students competing for 35 openings. Daisy is a fifth-grade student in East Los Angeles whose parents hope she can win a spot at KIPP LA PREP, where 135 students have applied for ten places. Emily is an eighth-grade student in Silicon Valley, where the local high school has gorgeous facilities, high graduation rates, and impressive test scores, but her family worries that she will be assigned to a slow track because of her low test scores; so they enter the lottery for Summit Preparatory Charter High School, where she is one of 455 students competing for 110 places.

The stars of the film are Geoffrey Canada, CEO of the Harlem Children's Zone, which provides a broad variety of social services to families and children and runs two charter schools; Michelle Rhee, then-chancellor of the Washington, DC, public school system, who closed schools, fired teachers and principals, and gained a national reputation for her tough policies; David Levin and Michael Feinberg, who have built a network of nearly 100 high-performing KIPP charter schools over the past 16 years; and Randi Weingarten, president of the American Federation of Teachers, who is cast in the role of chief villain. Other charter school leaders, like Steve Barr of the Green Dot chain in Los Angeles, do star turns, as does Bill Gates of Microsoft, whose foundation has invested many millions of dollars in expanding the number of charter schools. No successful public school teacher or principal or superintendent appears in the film; indeed there is no mention of any successful public school, only the incessant drumbeat of the theme of public school failure.

The situation is dire, the film warns us. We must act. But what must we do? The message of the film is clear. Public schools are bad; privately managed charter schools are good. Parents clamor to get their children out of the public schools in New York City (despite the claims by Mayor Michael Bloomberg that the city's schools are better than ever) and into the charters (the mayor also plans to double the number of charters, to help more families escape from the public schools that he controls). If we could fire the bottom 5 to 10% of the lowest performing teachers every year, says Hoover Institution economist Eric Hanushek in the film, our national test scores soon would approach the top of international rankings in mathematics and science.

Some fact-checking is in order, and the place to start is with the film's quiet acknowledgment that only one in five charter schools is able to get the "amazing results" that it celebrates. Nothing more is said about this astonishing statistic. It is drawn from a national study of charter schools by Stanford economist Margaret Raymond (the wife of Hanushek). Known as the CREDO study, it evaluated student progress on math tests in half the nation's 5,000 charter schools and concluded that 17% were superior to a matched traditional public school; 37% were worse than the public school; and the remaining 46% had academic gains no different from those of a similar public school. The proportion of charters that get amazing results is far smaller than 17%. Why did Davis Guggenheim pay no attention to the charter schools that are run by incompetent leaders or corporations concerned mainly with making money? Why propound to an unknowing public the myth that charter schools are the answer to our educational woes, when the filmmaker knows that there are twice as many failing charters as there are successful ones? Why not give an honest accounting?

The propagandistic nature of *Waiting for "Superman"* is revealed by Guggenheim's complete indifference to the wide variation among charter schools. There are excellent charter schools, just as there are excellent public schools. Why did he not also inquire into the charter chains that are mired in unsavory real estate deals, or take his camera to the charters where most students are getting lower scores than those in the neighborhood public schools? Why did he not report on the charter principals who have been indicted for embezzlement, or the charters that blur the line between church and state? Why did he not look into the charter schools whose leaders are paid $300,000–$400,000 a year to oversee small numbers of schools and students?

Guggenheim seems to believe that teachers alone can overcome the effects of student poverty, even though there are countless studies that demonstrate the link between income and test scores. He shows us footage of the pilot Chuck Yeager breaking the sound barrier, to the amazement of people who said it couldn't be done. Since Yeager broke the sound barrier, we should be prepared to believe that able teachers are all it takes to overcome the disadvantages of poverty, homelessness, joblessness, poor nutrition, absent parents, and so on.

The movie asserts a central thesis in today's school reform discussion: the idea that teachers are the most important factor determining student achievement. But this proposition is false. Hanushek has released studies showing that teacher quality accounts for about 7.5–10% of student test score gains. Several other high-quality analyses echo this finding, and while estimates vary a bit, there is a relative consensus: Teachers statistically account for around 10–20% of achievement outcomes. Teachers are the most important factor within schools.

But the same body of research shows that nonschool factors matter even more than teachers. According to University of Washington economist Dan Goldhaber, about 60% of achievement is explained by nonschool factors, such as family income. So while teachers are the most important factor within schools, their effects pale in comparison with those of students' backgrounds, families, and other factors beyond the control of schools and teachers. Teachers can have a profound effect on students, but it would be foolish to believe that teachers alone can undo the damage caused by poverty and its associated burdens.

Guggenheim skirts the issue of poverty by showing only families that are intact and dedicated to helping their children succeed. One of the children he follows is raised by a doting grandmother; two have single mothers who are relentless in seeking better education for them; two live with a mother and father. Nothing is said about children whose families are not available, for whatever reason, to support them, or about children who are homeless, or children with special needs. Nor is there any reference to the many charter schools that enroll disproportionately small numbers of children who are English-language learners or have disabilities.

The film never acknowledges that charter schools were created mainly at the instigation of Albert Shanker, president of the American Federation of Teachers from 1974 to 1997. Shanker had the idea in

1988 that a group of public school teachers would ask their colleagues for permission to create a small school that would focus on the neediest students, those who had dropped out and those who were disengaged from school and likely to drop out. He sold the idea as a way to open schools that would collaborate with public schools and help motivate disengaged students. In 1993, Shanker turned against the charter school idea when he realized that for-profit organizations saw it as a business opportunity and were advancing an agenda of school privatization. Michelle Rhee gained her teaching experience in Baltimore as an employee of Education Alternatives, Inc., one of the first of the for-profit operations.

Today, charter schools are promoted not as ways to collaborate with public schools but as competitors that will force them to get better or go out of business. In fact, charter schools have become the force for privatization that Shanker feared. Because of the high-stakes testing regime created by President George W. Bush's No Child Left Behind (NCLB) legislation, charter schools compete to get higher test scores than regular public schools and thus have an incentive to avoid students who might pull down their scores. Under NCLB, low-performing schools may be closed, while high-performing ones may get bonuses. Some charter schools "counsel out" or expel students just before state testing day. Some have high attrition rates, especially among lower performing students.

Perhaps the greatest distortion in this film is its misrepresentation of data about student academic performance. The film claims that 70% of eighth-grade students cannot read at grade level. This is flatly wrong. Guggenheim here relies on numbers drawn from the federally sponsored National Assessment of Educational Progress (NAEP). I served as a member of the governing board for the national tests for 7 years, and I know how misleading Guggenheim's figures are. NAEP doesn't measure performance in terms of grade-level achievement. The highest level of performance, "advanced," is equivalent to an A+, representing the highest possible academic performance. The next level, "proficient," is equivalent to an A or a very strong B. The next level is "basic," which probably translates into a C grade. The film assumes that any student below proficient is "below grade level." But it would be far more fitting to worry about students who are "below basic," who constitute 25% of the national sample, not 70%.

Guggenheim didn't bother to take a close look at the heroes of his documentary. Geoffrey Canada is justly celebrated for the creation of the Harlem Children's Zone, which not only runs two charter schools but surrounds children and their families with a broad array of social and medical services. Canada has a board of wealthy philanthropists and a very successful fundraising apparatus. With assets of more than $200 million, his organization has no shortage of funds. Canada himself currently is paid $400,000 annually. For Guggenheim to praise Canada, while also claiming that public schools don't need any more money, is bizarre. Canada's charter schools get better results than nearby public schools serving impoverished students. If all inner-city schools had the same resources as his, they might get the same good results.

But contrary to the myth that Guggenheim propounds about "amazing results," even Geoffrey Canada's schools have many students who are not proficient. On the 2010 state tests, 60% of the fourth-grade students in one of his charter schools and 50% in the other were not proficient in reading. It should be noted—and Guggenheim didn't note it—that Canada kicked out his entire first class of middle school students when they didn't get good enough test scores to satisfy his board of trustees. This sad event was documented by Paul Tough in his laudatory account of Canada's Harlem Children's Zone, *Whatever It Takes* (2009). Contrary to Guggenheim's mythology, even the best funded charters, with the finest services, can't completely negate the effects of poverty.

Guggenheim ignored other clues that might have gotten in the way of a good story. While blasting the teacher unions, he points to Finland as a nation whose educational system the United States should emulate, not bothering to explain that it has a completely unionized teaching force. His documentary showers praise on testing and accountability, yet he does not acknowledge that Finland seldom tests its students. Any Finnish educator will say that Finland improved its public education system not by privatizing its schools or constantly testing its students, but by investing in the preparation, support, and retention of excellent teachers. It achieved its present eminence not by systematically firing 5–10% of its teachers, but by patiently building for the future. Finland has a national curriculum, which is not restricted to the basic skills of reading and math, but includes the arts, sciences, history, foreign languages, and other subjects that are essential to a good, rounded education. Finland also strengthened its social welfare programs for children and families. Guggenheim simply ignores the realities of the Finnish system. Another significant difference overlooked by the film: Fewer than 4% of Finnish children live in poverty, as compared with more than 20% of American children.

In any school reform proposal, the question of "scalability" always arises. Can reforms be reproduced on a broad scale? The fact that one school produces amazing results is not in itself a demonstration that every other school can do the same. For example, Guggenheim holds up Locke High School in Los Angeles, part of the Green Dot charter chain, as a success story, but does not tell the whole story. With an infusion of $15 million of mostly private funding, Green Dot produced a safer, cleaner campus, but no more than tiny improvements in its students' abysmal test scores. According to the *Los Angeles Times*, the percentage of its students proficient in English rose from 13.7% in 2009 to 14.9% in 2010, while in math the proportion of proficient students grew from 4% to 6.7%. What can be learned from this slight progress? Becoming a charter is no guarantee that a school serving a tough neighborhood will produce educational miracles.

Another highly praised school that is featured in the film is the SEED charter boarding school in Washington, DC. SEED has been lauded by CBS's *60 Minutes* and others. It boasts remarkable rates of graduation and college acceptance. But SEED has a high attrition rate; of 140 students who entered the school in its early years, not more than a quarter graduated. SEED spends $35,000 per student, as compared with average current spending for public schools of about one-third that amount. Is our society prepared to open boarding schools for tens of thousands of inner-city students and pay what it costs to copy the SEED model? Those who claim that better education for the neediest students won't require more money, cannot use SEED to support their argument.

Guggenheim seems to demand that public schools start firing "bad" teachers so they can get the great results that one of every five charter schools gets. But he never explains how difficult it is to identify "bad" teachers. If one looks only at test scores, teachers in affluent suburbs get higher ones. If one uses student gains or losses as a general measure, then those who teach the neediest children— English-language learners, troubled students, autistic students—will see the smallest gains, and teachers will have an incentive to avoid districts and classes with large numbers of the neediest students.

Ultimately the job of hiring teachers, evaluating them, and deciding who should stay and who should go falls to administrators. We should be taking a close look at those who award due process rights (the accurate term for "tenure") to too many incompetent teachers. The best way to ensure that there are no bad or ineffective teachers in our public schools is to insist that we have principals and supervisors who are knowledgeable and experienced educators. Yet there is currently a vogue to recruit and train principals who have little or no education experience. (The George W. Bush Institute just announced its intention to train 50,000 new principals in the next decade and to recruit noneducators for this sensitive post.)

Waiting for "Superman" is the most important public relations coup that the critics of public education have made so far. Their power is not to be underestimated. For years, right-wing critics demanded vouchers and got nowhere. Now, many of them are watching in amazement as their ineffectual attacks on "government schools" and their advocacy of privately managed schools with public funding have become the received wisdom among liberal elites. Despite their uneven record, charter schools have the enthusiastic endorsement of the Obama administration, the Gates Foundation, the Broad Foundation, and the Dell Foundation. In recent months, *The New York Times* has published three stories about how charter schools have become the favorite cause of hedge fund executives. According to the *Times*, when Andrew Cuomo wanted to tap into Wall Street money for his gubernatorial campaign, he had to meet with the executive director of Democrats for Education Reform (DFER), a pro-charter group.

Dominated by hedge fund managers who control billions of dollars, DFER has contributed heavily to political candidates for local and state offices who pledge to promote charter schools. (Its efforts to unseat incumbents in three predominantly Black state senate districts in New York City came to nothing; none of its hand-picked candidates received as much as 30% of the vote in the primary elections, even with the full-throated endorsement of the city's tabloids.) Despite the loss of local elections and the defeat of Washington, DC, Mayor Adrian Fenty (who had appointed the controversial schools chancellor Michelle Rhee), the combined clout of these groups, plus the enormous power of the federal government and the uncritical support of the major media, presents a serious challenge to the viability and future of public education.

It bears mentioning that nations with high-performing school systems—whether Korea, Singapore, Finland, or Japan—have succeeded not by privatizing their schools or closing those with low scores, but by strengthening the education profession. They also have less poverty than we do. Fewer than 4% of children in Finland live in poverty, as compared with 20% in the United States. Those who insist that poverty doesn't matter, that only teachers matter, prefer to ignore such contrasts.

If we are serious about improving our schools, we will take steps to improve our teacher force, as Finland and other nations have done. That would mean better screening to select the best candidates, higher salaries, better support and mentoring systems, and better working conditions. Guggenheim complains that only one in 2,500 teachers loses his or her teaching certificate, but fails to mention that 50% of those who enter teaching leave within 5 years, mostly because of poor working conditions, lack of adequate resources, and the stress of dealing with difficult children and disrespectful parents. Some who leave "fire themselves"; others are fired before they get tenure. We also should insist that only highly experienced teachers become principals (the "head teacher" in the school), not retired businesspeople and military personnel. Every school should have a curriculum that includes a full range of studies, not just basic skills. And if we really are intent on school improvement, we must reduce the appalling rates of child poverty that impede success in school and in life.

There is a clash of ideas occurring in education right now between those who believe that public education is not only a fundamental right but a vital public service, akin to the public provision of police, fire protection, parks, and public libraries, and those who believe that the private sector is always superior to the public sector. *Waiting for "Superman"* is a powerful weapon on behalf of those championing the "free market" and privatization. It raises important questions, but all of the answers it offers require a transfer of public funds to the private sector. The stock market crash of 2008 should suffice to remind us that the managers of the private sector do not have a monopoly on success.

Public education is one of the cornerstones of American democracy. The public schools must accept everyone who appears at their doors, no matter their race, language, economic status, or disability. Like the huddled masses who arrived from Europe in years gone by, immigrants from across the world today turn to the public schools to learn what they need to know to become part of this society. The schools should be far better than they are now, but privatizing them is no solution.

In the final moments of *Waiting for "Superman,"* the children and their parents assemble in auditoriums in New York City, Washington, DC, Los Angeles, and Silicon Valley, waiting nervously to see whether they will win the lottery. As the camera pans the room, you see tears rolling down the cheeks of children and adults alike, all their hopes focused on a listing of numbers or names. Many people react to the scene with their own tears, sad for the children who lose. I had a different reaction. First, I thought to myself that the charter operators were cynically using children as political pawns in their own campaign to promote their cause. (Gail Collins in *The New York Times* had a similar reaction and wondered why they couldn't just send the families a letter in the mail instead of subjecting them to public rejection.) Second, I felt an immense sense of gratitude to the much-maligned American public education system, where no one has to win a lottery to gain admission.

CHAPTER 3

Educating Superman

Linda Darling-Hammond
Ann Lieberman

Good documentaries pick a powerful subject and engage viewers emotionally and intellectually in the subject at hand. In *Waiting for "Superman,"* Davis Guggenheim raptly engages the audience with the stories of five students and their parents who are struggling to find a good school. As observers, we connect to the 15 minutes spent on the lottery—and ache for the four students who don't get into the school of their choice. We feel a sense of conviction: It shouldn't be this way. All students should have a right to a good school! No one can be unaffected by the drama of these obviously deserving children and their anxious parents.

The story line—interwoven with a set of seemingly incontrovertible statistics—seems designed to leave viewers with the following conclusions:

- Public schools, especially those in urban areas, are uniformly failing.
- Money doesn't make a difference: Increases in spending on public schools have no effect on student achievement.
- Teacher unions are the major cause of this failure.
- Charter schools are the best solution to this problem, as they are more successful and less expensive.

While it succeeds on an emotional level, the documentary is, on an intellectual level, disingenuous, distorting and even dishonest in its misrepresentations of public education. The debate about school reform is framed by half-truths and distortions. The movie poses ideas in ways that are intended to suggest diagnoses or prescriptions for the problems it illustrates, and then drops them before they can be candidly considered or evaluated. For those who know something about educational research, the movie's intellectual story line personifies what Mark Twain had in mind when he quoted British Prime Minister Benjamin Disraeli as stating: "There are three kinds of lies: lies, damned lies, and statistics." *"Superman"* features all three. In an attempt to educate Superman, we take up some of the worst of these here.

1. PUBLIC SCHOOLS ARE UNIVERSALLY FAILING

"Superman" would have us believe that virtually all U.S. public schools—from wealthy suburbs to inner cities across the country— are failing and that the primary reasons are bad teaching and collective bargaining agreements that prevent change.

Never does the movie tell the story of public schools and systems that are succeeding. It does not point out that high-achieving states, like Massachusetts, Connecticut, and New Jersey, perform as well as the highest achieving nations in the world, with much more diverse student populations. Nor does it point out that these high-achieving states make strong investments in education and have undertaken purposeful systemic reforms to equalize access and to improve the quality of curriculum and teaching, as well as instructional resources, across schools and districts.[1]

The movie does not tell the story of growing childhood poverty and many states' unequal and inadequate school funding, which are the true villains of the American education story.

The reasons for concern are well known: Average student achievement in the United States lags behind other industrialized countries that have been making serious investments in their education systems. In 2009, the United States ranked 32nd out of the top 40 jurisdictions in mathematics, just above Portugal, and 30th in science, just above Spain, on the PISA tests.[2] While the United States performs closer to international averages in reading (ranking 24th, just after Latvia), scores dropped on the international reading tests during the No Child Left Behind era.

However, it is also true that, in 2009, U.S. schools with fewer than 10% of students in poverty ranked *first* among all nations in reading, while those serving more than 75% of students in poverty scored comparably to nations ranking about 50th.[3] And White and Asian students in the United States actually score above the OECD (Organization for Economic Cooperation and Development) average in every subject area, while African American and Hispanic students score so much lower that the national average plummets to the bottom tier of the rankings.[4]

What Guggenheim does not talk about is why these disparities exist. He does not explain that far more children (1 in 4) live in poverty in the United States than in any other industrialized nation, and far more lack basic supports—housing, health care, and food security—than in any of these nations. High-performing nations effectively have *all* of their students in schools with fewer than 10% of students in poverty, because they simply do not allow high levels of childhood neglect. Government supports ensure employment, housing, health care, and other basics for children, basics that are no longer provided by the tattered safety net that remains in the United States, as rates of severe poverty have grown to levels not seen since the Great Depression.

Furthermore, whereas high-achieving nations fund schools centrally and equally, the United States spends much more on the education of affluent children than of poor children, with wealthy suburbs often spending twice what central cities and three times what poor rural areas can afford.[5]

Both segregation of schools and inequality in funding have increased in many states over the past 2 decades, leaving a growing share of African American and Latino students in highly segregated apartheid schools that lack qualified teachers, up-to-date textbooks and materials, libraries, science labs, and computers, and safe, adequate facilities. Thus, the United States's poor standing is substantially a product of unequal access to quality education, the solution to which is to equitably fund public schools, rather than to abandon the system.

Guggenheim doesn't point out any of this, because acknowledging these very real issues would undermine his other major contentions: that teacher unions are the problem, and charter schools are the solution.

2. CHARTERS ARE THE SOLUTION

"Superman" presents the dilemma for students' families as one of getting out of bad public schools by getting into successful charter schools. The film includes four charter schools that it portrays as successful and no "regular" public schools that it indicates have done anything worthwhile. Certainly there are some successful and innovative schools that have been launched as charters. And certainly there are some charters that serve students with significant needs, without engaging in the selective admissions or push-out strategies that have caused concern about other charters' practices.[6]

Contrary to Guggenheim's assertion, these charters typically spend significantly more money, raised from private sources, than the public schools around them. Indeed, tens of millions of dollars beyond district funds have been spent on the Harlem Children's Zone, whose Promise Academies are featured in the movie. These funds for both schooling and comprehensive services for children have paid off over time, after the schools initially had a rocky start. They demonstrate that a whole-child approach is needed to support learning and long-term success.

And yet, national data show that extraordinarily successful charters are something of an anomaly. The largest study of charter schools, conducted by researchers at Stanford University's Hoover Institution, found that—across the 16 states included in the study—charters are about twice as likely to *underperform* regular public schools serving similar students as they are to outperform such schools. Only 17% of charters exceed the performance of regular public schools serving similar students; about 37% do significantly worse, and about 46% perform about the same.[7] Another carefully controlled national study of charter schools similarly found that when family background is controlled, district public schools outperform both private and charter schools.[8]

"Superman" would suggest that the solution to public school problems is to close "failing" public schools and replace them with schools that do not have to employ unionized teachers or report to publicly elected school boards. Yet a recent evaluation of Chicago's Renaissance 2010 initiative—which replaced a group of low-performing schools with new autonomous schools of choice, some of them charters or "contract schools" run by entrepreneurs or the district—found that the achievement of students in the new schools was no different from that of a matched comparison group of students in the old schools they had left, and that both groups continued to be very low-performing.[9]

More troubling is the fact that accountability pressures to get test scores up have led to growing concerns that many charters have raised their scores by excluding students who are most challenging to teach, either by structuring admissions so that low-achieving students and those with special education or other needs are unlikely to be admitted, or by creating conditions under which they are speedily encouraged to leave.[10]

In making its one-sided case, *"Superman"* ignores and even misrepresents data about public schools that are succeeding. For example, in seeking to promote Summit Academy—a very good charter school in Redwood City, California, in which our Stanford colleagues work closely with us—Guggenheim badly misrepresents a nearby public school that he seeks to portray as a grossly inadequate alternative. Woodside High School—also a school that partners with Stanford—is portrayed as a well-heeled school that produces mediocre results for an affluent student population. To create a stark contrast with Summit, the film suggests that, despite its advantages, Woodside fails to graduate many of its students and prepares relatively few for college.

"Superman" describes Woodside High School's appearance as that of a "private boarding school" in a community in which the average home price is $1.1 million. Had Guggenheim accepted the district's

invitation to learn more about the school, he would have discovered that Woodside actually serves a population that is 63% students of color and that about 40% of its students qualify for "free and reduced lunch"—a slightly higher proportion than at Summit, which serves a somewhat Whiter and wealthier student body. Furthermore, Woodside serves more than twice as many English learners as Summit and nearly twice as many students with disabilities, hosting Special Day classes for those with the most severe learning needs.

Yet both Summit and Woodside score a perfect "10" in the state accountability system, placing their test scores in the top 10% in the state, and both are ranked in *Newsweek's* 150 Top High Schools in the nation. Despite its more educationally needy student population, Woodside has a graduation rate of 96%, and 93% of students in its most recent graduating class planned to attend college. The remainder had plans to enter apprenticeships or the military, or to take a year off to travel before going on to college or careers.

Meanwhile, *"Superman"* includes none of the innovative public schools run by districts that have created new, successful models of education that outperform other public, private, and charter schools, despite reams of studies about many such schools. (In fact, many of the more recent charters borrowed their designs from these successful public school innovators.)

Take, for example, the group of innovative Boston Pilot schools, which are succeeding at rates far above those of many other schools serving similar students.[11] Or the more than 50 Coalition Campus schools developed in New York City in the early 1990s—long before charter schools had come on the horizon—which created designs that have been emulated all over the United States and the world. Schools like Vanguard, Landmark, and the Urban Academy, which replaced failing comprehensive high schools in Manhattan, continue to serve minority, low-income, and new immigrant students, graduating them far above city and state averages—and sending 80% or more on to college.

Take the many community schools that have been successful in cities like New York and Chicago, offering wraparound services to youth and families alongside high-quality instruction.[12] Take the

International High Schools network, which now has nearly a dozen high schools in New York, Boston, San Francisco, and Oakland, that serve new immigrants who enter not speaking English and leave well prepared, English-proficient, and en route to college. And take the many, many "regular" public schools in communities nationwide— including many cities—that have developed strong, successful programs that are the reasons for the statistics that find the schools, more often than not, more successful than charters serving similar students.

Guggenheim clearly had no interest in highlighting these schools, because improving education was not the goal of *"Superman."* Supporting a privatization agenda was.

3. MONEY DOESN'T MAKE A DIFFERENCE

While Guggenheim asserts, incorrectly, that charter schools are more successful and cost less than regular public schools, he also seeks to persuade the audience that money for schools is not the answer— despite the fact that he contrasts the costly private school his children attend with the much less attractive public school he passes every day on his way to drop them off.

One of the most striking graphics in *"Superman"* is one that appears to show that U.S. achievement trends have flatlined while dollar investments have increased. We do not know the source of that graphic, or the data on which it purportedly was based, but it misrepresents the reality of educational investments and achievement on at least two counts.

First, it fails to acknowledge that greater investments have supported enormous expansion of the public education system over the past half-century, in both size and diversity—and this expansion has resulted in huge gains in educational attainment. Public elementary and secondary schools grew from only 25 million students in 1950 to 49 million in 2010, with much greater participation by new immigrants, racial/ethnic minority students, and students with disabilities accounting for the increase. Until the 1960s, many communities did not even have high schools for Black students, Mexican American students, or American Indian students, and when they did, the schools were often segregated and severely underfunded. When that changed with desegregation, educational attainment jumped sharply. Between 1970 and 1998, the proportion of White adults who graduated from high school increased from just over 50% to 94%, and the proportion of Black adults who finished high school grew from 36% to 88%.[13]

Furthermore, until the Education for All Handicapped Children Act was passed in 1975, students with disabilities were not expected to attend school, and schools did not have to serve them. Enrollment of handicapped students leapt from near zero to close to 100%, with services starting at the age of 3 and extending to 21. Finally, between the 1960s and the turn of the 21st century, kindergarten enrollment became universal and 3- and 4-year-olds attending prekindergarten jumped from nearly nothing to more than 50%.[14]

Some of these funds have been spent to offset the growth of childhood poverty since the 1970s (nearly double now what it was then), which has required public schools to pick up costs for feeding students who don't get enough to eat at home, for health care, and for the social work services needed to support children and families who are falling through a tattered safety net. Funds also have been spent to support the burgeoning costs of health care both for children and for adults who work in schools; in many other countries with publicly supported health care systems, schools do not have to insure education employees or offer services to children.

Second, the *"Superman"* framing fails to report gains in achievement, especially for the newly included populations, over this time. The fact that gains were noticeable on both the NAEP and the SAT scores, even though the expanded population of students taking the tests was more educationally needy, means that the actual gains would have appeared higher had the population characteristics remained similar.

On the trend NAEP assessments, average mathematics scores were 24 points higher for 9-year-olds in 2008 than they were in 1973 (the first year of NAEP testing) and 15 points higher for 13-year-olds. And gains for Black students grew at more than double these rates, with increases of more than 50 and 45 points, respectively, for 9- and

13-year-olds. Latino students gained more than 35 points at each of these age levels. In reading, 9-year-olds gained 12 points between 1971 and 2008, and 13-year-olds gained 5 points. Here, too, gains for Black and Latino students were more than double White rates.[15]

These gains have occurred in recent years despite growing inequality in funding for rich and poor schools since the late 1980s. During the 1960s and 1970s, when federal investments were greatest in poor urban and rural schools, the Black–White achievement gap in reading decreased by about 75%. Had the policies that supported school funding equalization, desegregation, and investments in high-quality teaching for high-need schools not been rolled back in the 1980s when federal funds for education were cut in half, this progress would have eliminated the racial achievement gap by the year 2000.

Equally important, Guggenheim does not tell the story of the dramatic gains in achievement that have occurred in states that finally have addressed these disparities. In the late 1980s and early 1990s, states like Connecticut, Massachusetts, and North Carolina undertook reforms, on the heels of equity lawsuits, that both equalized resources to school districts and dramatically improved teaching.[16] More recently, New Jersey became one of the highest achieving states in the nation (ranked first in writing and among the top five states in every other area assessed by the NAEP) and closed its achievement gap by half, by reducing inequities in funding with a purposeful plan for school investments and reform.[17]

New Jersey fought school funding lawsuits for more than 30 years and finally, in 1998, implemented parity funding for the 30 low-income urban districts that had long spent half of what wealthy suburbs like Princeton and New Brunswick could spend. The state implemented high-quality preschool in these *Abbott* districts,[18] accompanied by widespread teacher training, intensive professional development in literacy and, later, mathematics to support curriculum improvements, investments in instructional materials, wraparound services for students in high-need communities, and increases in educator salaries and quality in these high-need districts. In addition to its high levels of achievement, New Jersey also has the highest graduation rates in the nation, including those for African American males, which are far above national averages.[19] With a highly diverse student population—45% students of color and more than one third of children living in poverty—New Jersey demonstrates that thoughtfully made investments in education can enable a systemic reform that pays off for all its children.

4. WE COULD SOLVE AMERICA'S CRISIS IF WE FOLLOWED FINLAND'S EXAMPLE

Finally, the film notes that Finland is the highest ranked OECD country with respect to international education comparisons, and suggests that the U.S. economy would be much improved if it followed Finland's example. Here, Guggenheim has it partly right. Finland has indeed created one of the most successful education systems in the world. It routinely ranks as one of the world's highest achieving and most equitable nations on the international PISA tests, even though it once had a decidedly mediocre and very inequitable system. (Fifty years ago, with only 10% of adults having finished more than 9 years of basic education, Finland's level of educational attainment was closer to that of Malaysia or Peru, rather than its Scandinavian neighbors.[20])

However, Guggenheim has it completely wrong if he thinks his film's prescriptions have anything to do with Finland's successful strategy for reform. Indeed, Finland's approach is the polar opposite of what the United States has been doing, or what *Waiting for "Superman"* would suggest we should do more of.

Finland has no charter schools, no vouchers, and no funding inequities. It also has almost no poverty—all of its children have access to housing, health care, and food security. Finland has a well-funded, highly equitable public education system serving nearly 100% of its students—a system that hires some of the best trained and most highly unionized teachers in the world. All of its teachers attend top-quality teacher education programs at the graduate level, completely at government expense, and with a stipend while they train.[21] Because the nation has invested in ensuring that all of its teachers are well prepared, Finland has no agenda to fire bad teachers. And it has not eliminated teacher tenure or the importance of seniority.

Contrary to the advice of economist Eric Hanushek, one of our Stanford colleagues who suggests that if the United States were to eliminate the bottom 10% of teachers, it could raise U.S. education achievement to Finnish levels, we cannot fire our way to Finland. Indeed, Finnish policy analyst Pasi Sahlberg notes,

> There is no formal teacher evaluation in Finland. Teachers receive feedback from their principal and the school staff itself. . . . Once a teacher has permanent employment in a school, there are no checkpoints or means for terminating a contract unless there is a violation of the ethical rules of teaching. Finland relies on the strong preparation of teachers, their professional ethic, and their opportunities for ongoing engagement with colleagues in the professional work of teaching and curriculum and assessment development to support their effectiveness. . . . When new teachers are employed in a school, they usually stay there for life.[22]

Finland also does not try to motivate teachers by merit pay: The single salary schedule is designed to ensure that salaries are competitive with other occupations and essentially equal (with small additional stipends to attract teachers to sparsely populated rural schools). Teachers are expected to collaborate, not to compete with one another. They are not rewarded or punished based on student test scores. In fact, Finland has no mandated external tests for students at all, with the exception of the voluntary matriculation exam for college in 12th grade—which is written by high school and university faculty together. It is the strong preparation, support, trust, and autonomy that teachers are granted that is the secret to Finland's success. Sahlberg points out,

> Teachers compare what they do in a primary school classroom to the work that doctors do in medical clinics. A key characteristic of Finnish teachers' work environment is that they are autonomous, trusted, and respected professionals. Unlike nations that have bureaucratic account-

ability systems that make teachers feel threatened, over-controlled, and undervalued, teaching in Finland is a very sophisticated profession, where teachers feel they can truly exercise the skills they have learned in the university. Test-based accountability is replaced by shared responsibility and inspiration for human development.[23]

A MORE-GROUNDED PERSPECTIVE

If we actually want to create high-quality schools for all children in the United States, our strategies should emulate the best of what has been accomplished in public education both here and abroad. While there is considerable talk about international test score comparisons in U.S. policy circles, there is too little talk about what high-performing countries actually *do*: fund schools equitably; pay teachers competitively and comparably; invest in high-quality preparation, mentoring, and professional development for teachers and leaders, completely at government expense; organize a curriculum around problem-solving and critical thinking skills; and test students rarely—and almost never with multiple-choice tests. Indeed, the top-performing nations increasingly rely on school-based assessments of learning that include challenging projects, investigations, and performances, much like what leading educators have created in the innovative public schools we mentioned earlier.

While charter schools may be a small part of a broader strategy, they cannot substitute for building an effective and equitable public school system. To create this system, we must pursue short- and long-term strategies for change that include:

- A renewed commitment to the health and welfare of American families, including a new War on Poverty, investments in employment, and universal health care.
- Community schools that can offer the wraparound services needed to support whole-child development and success for a fraction of the cost of ventures like the Harlem Children's Zone, and with more possibility of widespread scale-up.

- Equitable funding of public schools, so that all children start from a level playing field. Such funding would start from a platform of equal dollars per pupil, adjusted for cost-of-living differentials and pupil needs, adding a weighted allocation for students living in poverty, new English learners, and those with disabilities.
- Elimination of the structural barriers that prevent regular public schools from innovating and creating ever more successful learning opportunities for all students. These include the hyper-regulation of schools by state agencies and local districts, as well as the renegotiation of collective bargaining agreements that were developed by both unions and school boards in the era of factory-model education.
- High-quality preparation and leadership development programs for teachers and principals that are offered free of charge—as in high-performing countries—to all members of the profession in exchange for a service commitment to the public education system.
- Mentoring programs for all new teachers and principals, offered by expert veterans who are trained and have released time for this purpose, as is common in high-achieving nations.
- Time incorporated into the school schedule for collaborative planning and ongoing professional learning to continually improve instruction, as is common in other countries (typically 15–25 hours per week).
- Support for teachers to participate in professional networks, like the National Writing Project, which allow them to share and develop effective practices with one another.
- A 21st-century curriculum and assessment system that offers lean curriculum guidance (i.e., less prescriptive and more general in nature), focuses on critical thinking and problem solving, and engages in performance assessments that both measure learning and inform teaching productively.

The United States has a long history of "reform," which has become an almost constant process. We need stop "reforming" and become smart and honest about what kinds of educational strategies actually work—and we need to stop chasing silver bullets and shibboleths if we are to create genuine educational opportunity for all students. We have learned over and over again the harmful effects of top-down, poorly informed reforms: They demoralize the staff, frustrate the community, and leave people feeling helpless rather than hopeful.

There is a very robust change literature in education that demonstrates the powerful effects of collaboration, rather than competition, both within schools and across schools—of building individual and collective capacities so that good teaching becomes widespread and learning occurs throughout the system.

If American public education is to improve, we will need to support, rather than blame, our teachers, who have taken on one of the hardest jobs in the world; collaborate with teachers' organizations that must help create systemic reforms, rather than make them the sole scapegoats for low test scores that are largely a product of other policies; and fight to protect and improve the public schools that must serve our democracy. There is no other way to find Superman.

NOTES

1. For an account of such reforms, see L. Darling-Hammond, *The Flat World and Education: How America's Commitment to Equity Will Determine Our Nation's Future* (New York: Teachers College Press, 2010).

2. OECD, *PISA 2009 Results: What Students Know and Can Do—Student Performance in Reading, Mathematics and Science*, vol. 1 (2010): http://dx.doi.org/10.1787/9789264091450-en.

3. Ibid.

4. Darling-Hammond, *Flat World*.

5. Ibid.

6. D. Friedlaender and L. Darling-Hammond, *High Schools for Equity*. (http://www.srnleads.org/press/pdfs/hsfe_report.pdf)

7. M. Raymond, *Multiple Choice* (Stanford: Center for Research on Educational Outcomes, Hoover Institution, 2009).

8. C. Lubienski and S. Lubienski, "School Sector and Academic Achievement: A Multi-Level Analysis of NAEP Mathematics Data," *American Educational Research Journal* 43, no. 4 (2006): 651–698.

9. L. Cassidy, D. Humphrey, M. Wechsler, and V. Young, *High School Reform in Chicago Public Schools: Renaissance 2010* (Menlo Park, CA: SRI International, 2009).

10. R. Chait and M. McLaughlin, *Realizing the Promise: How State Policy Can Support Alternative Certification Programs* (Washington, DC: Center for American Progress, 2009).

11. D. French, "Boston's Pilot Schools: An Alternative to Charter Schools," in *Keeping the Promise: The Debate Over Charter Schools,* 67–80 (Milwaukee, WI: Rethinking Schools, 2008).

12. D. Kirp, "Cradle to College," *The Nation*, June 14, 2010: http://www.thenation.com/article/cradle-college; ICF International, *Communities in Schools National Evaluation: Five Year Summary Report* (Fairfax, VA: Author, 2010).

13. National Center for Education Statistics (NCES), *Digest of Education Statistics, 1999* (Washington, DC: U.S. Department of Education, 2000), 17.

14. Ibid., 15.

15. B. D. Rampey, G. S. Dion, and P. L. Donahue, *The Nation's Report Card: Trends in Academic Progress in Reading and Mathematics, 2008* (Washington, DC: National Center for Education Statistics, 2009), http://nces.ed.gov/nationsreportcard/pubs/main2008/2009479.asp.

16. *Flat World*, chap. 5.

17. Ibid., chap. 4.

18. In 1985, the ruling of *Abbott v. Burke* ruled that public schools in poor communities were unconstitutionally substandard. These "Abbott districts" were provided resources to bring the quality of education up to standard.

19. M. Holzman, *Yes We Can: The Schott 50 State Report on Public Education and Black Males 2010* (Cambridge, MA: Schott Foundation for Public Education, 2010).

20. P. Sahlberg, "Developing Effective Teachers and School Leaders: The Case of Finland," in *Teacher and Leader Effectiveness in High-Performing Education Systems*, eds. Linda Darling-Hammond and Robert Rothman (Washington, DC: Alliance for Excellent Education and Stanford: Stanford Center for Opportunity Policy in Education, 2011).

21. Darling-Hammond, *Flat World*.

22. Sahlberg, "Developing Effective Teachers," 16.

23. Ibid.

CHAPTER 4

The Potential Impact of *Waiting for "Superman"* on Schooling in America

Arthur Levine

Waiting for "Superman" is a call to action for the nation, which, if successful, would result in the closure of bad schools, the availability of high-quality schools for all children, the firing of weak teachers, the hiring of strong teachers, and the elimination of the obstacles that prevent these changes. The question is, what kind of impact is *Waiting for "Superman"* likely to have on schooling in America?

AN ERA OF CHANGE

We live in a time of profound, swift, and continuing change—demographic, economic, technological, and global. Demographically, America is aging, facing a tidal wave of retirements, changing color, taking on new immigrants from abroad, and moving from cities to suburbs and from the north and east to the Sunbelt, with an attendant movement from blue to red politics.

Economically, the country is shifting from an industrial to a knowledge-based economy. In the transition, low-education jobs and entire industries are disappearing. They are being replaced by information industry jobs that require higher levels of skill and knowledge than ever before in history. This entails a shift from a focus on process, exemplified by the assembly line, which industrial societies require, to an emphasis on outcomes, assessment, and accountability, which information economies demand. In this environment, wealth is being redistributed so that the rich are getting much richer and the poor and middle class are getting poorer.

Technologically and globally, the United States is inextricably intertwined in a digital world of instantaneous communications, news, data, and finances in which new technologies have reshaped seemingly every aspect of our lives—from how we work, date, and bank to how we shop, read, and entertain ourselves. Revolutions can be kindled by Twitter.

All of our social institutions—government, health care, media, finance, and education—were created for a different time and a world that is dying. None of these systems work as well as they once did, it seems, and all appear to be broken today. They need to be refitted for a new era. The nation is responding in two ways— attempting to fix current institutions while simultaneously seeking to replace them.

These are the new realities operating in our schools. In an information economy in which low-level manufacturing jobs are moving abroad, there is no longer a place for high school dropouts, traditionally regarded as a cost of doing business. In a high-technology society in which good jobs require greater levels of education than ever before, high school graduation standards are being raised. The historic assembly line model of schooling, with its focus on common processes—13 years of schooling by age group for 180 days a year from 8 a.m. to 3 p.m. with classes for lengths of time prescribed by the Carnegie Foundation in 1910—is giving way to an emphasis on common outcomes, entailing the adoption of common standards, assessment regimens, and accountability requirements. The currency of schooling is shifting from teaching to learning. This means that our technology-rich, outcome-based, accountability-driven system of schooling is now charged with educating all of the children in the most diverse generation in U.S. history to the highest levels of skills and knowledge ever required in order to prepare them for life in a global information economy. Toward this end, the nation is moving at once to reform the existing schools and invent new ones.

Reforming the Nation's Schools. Since 1983 and the release of the report *A Nation at Risk*, the United States has been undergoing an education reform movement involving government at all levels, our schools and colleges, unions, the media, philanthropy, special interest groups, professional associations, political parties, researchers, pundits, the business community, the public, and just about any other group one can imagine. The rhetoric often has been superheated, driven more frequently by ideology than empirical data, and by the wants of adults more than the needs of children. The focus and methods of reform have varied dramatically and continuously, too often embracing the fad du jour. Today the search for a silver bullet continues. So do reports of the United States lagging behind other nations in academic performance and the achievement gap, the disparity in our children's academic performance by race, geography, and family income.

The reform movement has taken two directions. One is the fixing of broken schools and school systems. The spotlight has been on a relatively small number of principals and superintendents, such as Joel Klein and Michelle Rhee, who have been bold in leading the nation's more than 13,500 school districts and nearly 96,000 public schools. However, after more than a quarter century of a reform movement, not one major urban school district has been successfully turned around.

The other is occurring at the periphery of the existing schools. It accepts the current time-based, assembly-line model of schooling, but seeks to improve those schools by changing specific aspects of schooling. Examples of these initiatives are Teach for America, which focuses on improving the schools by raising the quality of teacher candidates and changing the way in which they are prepared; charter school organizations, such as Mosaic and Green Dot, which believe that schools can be strengthened by changing the way in which they are governed; and KIPP, which holds that changing the calendar and curriculum at schools will change their performance. Today there are more than 8,200 Teach for America volunteers annually teaching 500,000 students; 5,500 charter schools in 40 states enrolling more than 1.5 million students; and 99 KIPP schools in 20 states enrolling 27,000 students.

When successful, school reform initiatives are ameliorative, producing more strong schools and reducing the number of failing schools.

Replacing the Nation's Schools. Change here is based in the belief that today's schools are fundamentally flawed and need to be reinvented. The key elements of change have been a shift in emphasis from teaching to learning, from process to outcomes, from fixed to variable time, and from one-size-fits-most to individualized education for each.

This sector is tiny; it pales in size and funding when compared with school reform initiatives. It has received financial support from several innovation-minded foundations, including the Kauffman and MacArthur Foundations. It has been fueled by authors such as Clayton Christensen, Howard Gardner, and Mel Levine. It has so far produced a small number of new schools such as Quest to Learn and School of One. The goal in this sector is systemic change.

In the years ahead, given the record of school reform initiatives, the replacement sector is likely to grow, with increased funding and expansion in the number of replacement schools, which should become stronger and more mature with successive iterations. In the long run, this sector could well become the dominant model of schooling as failing traditional schools are closed, the ranks of replacements grow, and funding and regulation shift to the new sector that encapsulates the values of the information age. Performance and cost will be determinants.

***The Impact of* Waiting for "Superman."** *Waiting for "Superman"* deals wholly with school reform. It is silent on the issue of school replacement, which is not an omission but an affirmation of Davis Guggenheim's confidence that reform can do the job. In this sense, *Waiting for "Superman"* is a part of America's long history and tradition of reform-minded publications, television documentaries, and movies. It joins the company of books, fiction and nonfiction, such as Harriet Beecher Stowe's *Uncle Tom's Cabin*, Upton Sinclair's *The Jungle*, Rachel Carson's *Silent Spring*, and Ralph Nader's *Unsafe at Any Speed*. It follows the road of Edward R. Murrow's documentaries on Senator Joseph McCarthy and his tactics, and movies such as *Gentleman's Agreement* and Davis Guggenheim's earlier film, *An Inconvenient Truth*.

What has been the impact of these works? Change occurs in a series of stages: (a) recognizing a problem; (b) publicizing the problem and generating public concern; (c) formulating solutions to the problem and placing the problem and solutions on the agenda of key policymakers, practitioners, and stakeholders; (d) creating a coalition of policymakers, practitioners, and stakeholders; (e) gaining approval for the solutions; and (f) implementing and institutionalizing the solutions.

Each of the documentaries and docudramas mentioned had similar effects. They focused on problems that had been recognized earlier. They vividly spotlighted, publicized, and generated public concern about the issues—slavery, the meat and automobile industries, the environment, anti-Semitism, and government misconduct. Most succeeded as well in placing the issue on the desks of the key players required for action. In each case, change followed, but not as a direct consequence of the book, program, or film. The primary effect of these works was to turn up the heat on a recognized social problem.

THE FLEXNER REPORT:
AN EXAMPLE OF COMPREHENSIVE EDUCATION REFORM

In education, one volume, *On Medical Education in the United States and Canada*, went much further. It is credited with dramatically raising the quality of the nation's doctors, their preparation for the medical profession, and the outcomes of their work. The study was sponsored by the Carnegie Foundation for the Advancement of Teaching in 1910 and carried out by a young educator named

Abraham Flexner, recommended by Charles Eliot, the president of Harvard. Flexner visited every medical school in the United States and Canada, wrote a report that established standards for medical education, identified model medical schools that already demonstrated the standards, offered recommendations for improving the quality of medical schools, and provided an assessment of every medical school in North America.

Known as the "Flexner Report," it had the effect of remaking medical education, closing the country's poorest medical schools, strengthening weaker schools, and investing in excellent schools. It resulted in raised AMA standards for doctors and medical education, more rigorous state certification requirements, an outpouring of private and public funding for medicine and medical education, more rigorous admission standards for students entering medical school, and improved quality of medical services in the country. The report was not the first to recognize the problem of poor medical education and it certainly could not ensure the institutionalization of the changes it proposed.

The success of the Flexner initiative is attributed by historians to eight factors:

1. The timing was right. There was broad dissatisfaction with the quality of doctors, medical education, and medical services in the United States.
2. The right organization was sponsoring the effort. The Carnegie Foundation for the Advancement of Teaching had the standing, prestige, board of trustees, benefactor, and relationship with universities to make the work visible, important, and credible.
3. The research was comprehensive, clear, and undeniable.
4. In the performance of the German universities and the Johns Hopkins medical school, the study was afforded demonstrable models of medical excellence from which to establish expectations and needed standards of practice.
5. The recommendations were straightforward, grounded in research, and targeted at specific stakeholders.

6. The networks of key stakeholders were created at the start of the project to build awareness, ownership, and willingness to act. These included the profession via the AMA, educators by means of the best medical schools, the press, government, and funders.

7. There was wide dissemination of the research. Fifteen thousand copies of the report were distributed to the key actors and the press campaign was unprecedented.

8. In the aftermath of the research, the Carnegie Foundation mobilized the actors needed to carry out change—the AMA, state government and licensing boards, and foundations, particularly the Rockefeller Foundation. In the years after the Flexner Report, foundations gave over $150 million to improve medical education, the equivalent of billions today.

Waiting for "Superman" did quite a few of these things. The times were certainly right. America was a quarter century into a school reform movement. The President of the United States and his Secretary of Education were advocating and funding a reform agenda, not dissimilar from Guggenheim's. Governors viewed the future of their states, making the transition from industrial to information economies, as dependent upon education. The achievement gap tenaciously continued, and the United States lagged behind other nations in international comparisons. The changes Guggenheim urged were on the ascendancy—charter schools, access to quality schools, teaching excellence, and accountability.

Guggenheim brought a reputation for powerful documentary with *An Inconvenient Truth*, but not the dispassionate reputation of Carnegie. The story he told was powerful, but more a matter of opinion than "impartial" research. Guggenheim pointed out examples of success, although more controversial than Flexner's. His recommendations were clear, but discrete rather than comprehensive. The dissemination was broad, on a scale far beyond what was possible, even imaginable, for the Flexner Report. The press was extraordinary: pre-release, opening, and post-release. The discussion of the film filled the blogosphere. It was impossible for policymakers, practitioners, or stakeholders to overlook or to avoid taking a stand on *Waiting for "Superman."*

There were larger and more consequential differences. For a report or documentary to achieve systemic change, there are four necessary, but insufficient, steps. First, create a national debate. If the documentary receives major press coverage, it kicks off a national debate on the topic and the merits of its case involving the key actors, stakeholders, and the public. If credible in content and authorship, the more controversial the documentary, the louder the reaction is likely to be.

Second, speak to power. If a documentary is highly visible, much discussed, and a subject of national concern, the author is invited to speak to, testify before, and counsel policymakers and practitioners and their professional associations.

Third, participate in/witness serendipitous change. Pieces of the documentary—recommendations, examples of best practice, or assessment tools—are adopted or used in one fashion or another by states, cities, school districts, schools, universities, commissions, or other policymakers or practitioners. Sometimes the author is aware of these initiatives and sometimes not. Sometimes the author is involved and sometimes not. Sometimes the change is sincere and sometimes not. Sometimes the attribution to the documentary is accurate and sometimes it is spurious.

Fourth, organize for systemic change. Systemic change requires the identification of a governance unit that has the capacity to adopt comprehensive change and the creation of a coalition of the key actors across that community necessary to carry out comprehensive change. An example would be to focus on a state as a whole and creating a coalition consisting of the governor, key legislators on both sides of the aisle, the state school board and chief state school officer, the state higher education executive officer and board, the universities and school districts, unions, businesses, and philanthropists. Without the targeting and coalition building, all that is possible is piecemeal change.

THE FLEXNER REPORT AND *WAITING FOR "SUPERMAN"*

Waiting for "Superman" accomplished the first three. The Carnegie Foundation achieved all four. The consequence is that the Flexner Report resulted in systemic change and *Waiting for "Superman"* is likely to produce piecemeal and serendipitous changes.

However, *Waiting for "Superman"* has attributes that the Carnegie Foundation lacked. The audience that it reached is geometrically larger than the Flexner Report's. In addition, concern with school improvement is a more popular issue than medical education.

But the most important difference is the Internet, which did not exist in the age of Flexner. It has been the foundation of the *Waiting for "Superman"* strategy. There is a website, a Twitter feed, a Facebook page, texting, an iPad app, a concert with major artists, a book, a DVD, house parties, public showings of the film, town hall meetings, alliances with foundations and not-for-profit organizations, suggestions for citizen action, and local movements in 30 cities, among other things. *Waiting for "Superman"* has taken an entirely different approach to change than the Carnegie Foundation. Its focus is on the grassroots, launching a popular movement for school reform.

We have seen powerful initiatives of this type in recent years. Barack Obama's campaign for the presidency was fueled by social media, and Twitter had a profound impact on revolutionary movements in the Mideast.

Waiting for "Superman" is seeking to create this movement at a critical moment. The rift between political parties on so many issues is much less pronounced in education. Although Republicans are more likely to champion vouchers and publicly chastise teacher unions, there is substantial agreement on the need to expand the number of charter schools; end last hired, first fired policies; ease the removal of failing teachers; adopt pay for performance; use test data on student learning to evaluate teacher performance; and improve the quality of teacher preparation. When the Obama administration came to office, it radically changed the education agenda of the nation, adopting a number of policies such as these, which previously had been regarded as Republican. These are also the issues that were highlighted in *Waiting for "Superman"* and it means that view by view, tweet by tweet, text by text, house party by house party, this film has the potential to heat up and accelerate the existing school reform movement and bring about more reform for more schools and more children.

The bottom line is that *Waiting for "Superman"* will not further the replacement of the current model of schooling, and will not bring about the systemic change of our schools, but it has the promise of fueling and expanding the current school reform movement and the approaches that have gained currency in recent years. It is likely to accomplish this in three ways. First, by putting a spotlight on the problems it identified and the solutions it proposed, the film promises to build public awareness and support for action. Second, by giving encouragement and legitimacy to current advocates proposing comparable solutions, the movie is likely to spur further action in a more hospitable climate. Third, by documenting the urgency of the problem and demonstrating the efficacy of the solutions it proposes, *Waiting for "Superman"* has the potential to expand the pool of policy and practice actors who are already seeking solutions, looking for silver bullets, and likely to embrace *Superman's* proposals as those silver bullets. This is an extraordinary accomplishment for a movie, putting it in a class with works such as *Silent Spring*, the Murrow documentaries, and *An Inconvenient Truth*. Its long-term importance will be a matter for historians to judge.

CHAPTER 5

Newsflash: Superman Has Arrived! And He's Brought an Army

Milton Chen

Waiting for "Superman" must be the most talked-about documentary about schools in recent years. In my three viewings of it, I came to value it more and more, especially for bringing the desperate plight of American public education to the attention of a larger audience. As critical as schools are to our democracy, we have done a very poor job of educating the public about public education, its present, and its future. At the NBC Education Nation conference at Rockefeller Center in September 2010, the screening of *Waiting for "Superman"* put faces on the plight of inner-city children and parents who desperately know that a high-quality education is their ticket to success but repeatedly come up empty-handed.

THE POWER OF VISUAL STORYTELLING

The great movements for social change succeed not just through reports from blue-ribbon panels, but reach their tipping point when we tell ourselves the stories of those affected and when those stories involve emotionally moving visual images. During the 1960s, photos of freedom marchers in the Deep South being power-hosed and attacked by police dogs, and scenes of Vietnamese children running naked from their napalm-burned villages transformed our consciousness about civil rights and the war in Vietnam. More recently, images of glaciers melting in *An Inconvenient Truth*, also directed by Davis Guggenheim, provided powerful visual evidence of climate change. Now, the heartwrenching stories Guggenheim has told about Anthony, Bianca, Daisy, Emily, and Francisco are part of our collective memory whenever we think about urban schools.

Still, *Waiting for "Superman,"* like so many policy debates, focuses on the structure of school systems and problems with teacher quality. The scenes of long-suffering families waiting, and waiting some more, to be selected in charter school lotteries make the case for the flexibility and site-based management of charter schools. The film also devotes much screen time to sanctions for poor teachers, highlighting Michelle Rhee's "take no prisoners" firings in Washington, DC.

However, the issues of charter schools and firing poor teachers have been with us for more than 20 years. The Superman metaphor itself hearkens back to an even earlier age of comic books and black-and-white TV. In fact, *Waiting for "Superman"* could have been made in 1990. And we might be further along in the path to school reform if it had. But these two apparent solutions don't address the larger central problem: the need to create entirely different types of schools for the learning that students need in these fast-changing times.

DESIGNING SCHOOLS FOR THE 21ST CENTURY

One weekday afternoon, a friend of mine saw her 13-year-old son in front of the TV with his cell phone on and laptop open. She complained to him that he couldn't possibly be doing his homework. She could see him typing into multiple Facebook and Google screens, while texting and watching TV. Without looking up, he said, "Mom, we're in a different era." We're indeed living in a different age, where the information students need to sift through and analyze is on the

Internet, not contained between the covers of their textbooks or their teachers' ears.

In the film, Geoffrey Canada recalls his boyhood hope that, someday, Superman—"faster than a speeding bullet, more powerful than a locomotive"—might land in his midst to save the day and his community. Alas, there would be no superhero, and the hard work of changing the schools would be left to courageous individuals—like Canada himself—who would fight the good fight, one school and one district at a time.

In fact, there have always been many superheroes working miracles in their own schools. Importantly, they are making changes from the inside out, starting at the classroom level, changing the specific behaviors of teachers and students in 21st-century classrooms. But these local heroes are much less well known than Geoffrey Canada. It would help tremendously if TV networks, still able to command audiences of millions, would devote more airtime to their stories, just as 60 Minutes brought Canada and the Harlem Children's Zone to national attention. We can only hope that the Fox network will create a show called American Teacher Idol to generate the same kind of national mania it does for amateur singers.

YOUTUBE CAN BE AN EDUTUBE

But it's not much use Waiting for Fox, either. And now, we don't need to. YouTube, which turns a young 6 years old in 2012, along with other video-sharing sites, has been an extraordinary boon to the movement to share images of innovative classrooms. In mathematics alone—from inspiring TED Talks, such as high school teacher and doctoral student Dan Meyer's talk on math instruction (http://www.ted.com/talks/dan_meyer_math_curriculum_makeover.html) to Khan Academy's brief tutorials on mathematics (http://www.khanacademy.org/)—we now have a critical mass of tools to make us smarter about what powerful learning looks and feels like in the classroom. Dan Meyer and Sal Khan are just two individuals demonstrating the "power of one" in the Internet Age and how local innovators can achieve global audiences. Their videos show how math education can be improved not just someday, but Monday.

Our work at the George Lucas Educational Foundation also has pursued this strategy of "inside out" reform by filming teachers who have persisted, often against great odds, in designing classrooms for students' futures rather than teachers' pasts. Our first story, dating back to 1997, featured Jim Dieckmann, a grade school teacher in Chula Vista, California, who understood the potential of the Internet and organized a project for students to collect insects in their backyards and schoolyards. The insects were sent to entomologists at nearby San Diego State University. The students videoconferenced with the scientists and were able to see their insects under the university's electron microscope. One of our most popular films to this day follows the 2002 story of Eeva Reeder, who invited school architects into her 10th-grade geometry classroom near Seattle to mentor her students in a design competition, using Computer-Aided Design (CAD) software to design schools of the future.

Over 15 years, the Edutopia website (edutopia.org) has become a repository of films on more than 150 innovative schools and thousands of courageous teachers and principals, from High Tech High in San Diego to Intel Schools of Distinction to the Maine middle school laptop program. These classrooms show students engaged in project-based learning, for instance, monitoring species and sharing their data online, as in the Journey North or Nature Mapping programs, or using geographic information systems in the Environmental and Spatial Technologies (EAST) program to study the archaeology and history of their communities. EAST students at Horace Mann Magnet Middle School in Arkansas made multimedia stories of Japanese internment camps nearby and traveled to California to interview survivors. These stories have been curated and published in three books.[1]

SOCIAL/EMOTIONAL LEARNING:
A CRITICAL PART OF A 21ST-CENTURY CURRICULUM

Edutopia documentaries have advocated for inclusion of social/emotional learning (SEL) as the "other side of the curriculum." A recent *New York Times Magazine* article entitled "What If the

Secret to Success Is Failure?" highlighted the importance of social/ emotional skills as part of the solution when KIPP schools faced the finding that only 33% of their middle school graduates went on to complete college.[2] Success in high school, college, and beyond turned out to rely not only on academic skill but on something more important but much less valued in schools, what author Paul Tough deemed "character." The skills of persistence and resilience and the abilities to communicate and work well with others are becoming the most valuable currency in the new economy of college and career success.

These skills are not just a matter of a student's temperament and family background, but, like academic skills, can be developed and improved. SEL curricula demonstrate that these skills can and should be taught to students, and the earlier, the better. Two of the best districts implementing SEL programs are in Anchorage and Louisville. Edutopia profiled the Anchorage program, led by Superintendent Carol Comeau, in 2007, showing how SEL can help students identify and manage their emotions and improve their communication skills. As Comeau points out in the Edutopia film, Alaska had the nation's highest per capita rate of domestic violence and child abuse. With about 50,000 students, Anchorage is one of the largest 100 districts in the country, a majority minority district with 9% Alaskan Native and American Indian students, where 94 languages are spoken, most commonly Spanish, Hmong, Tagalog, Samoan, and Korean.

The district's program, Change of Heart, emphasizes active listening, not only when conflicts arise, on the playground and in the classroom, but in the curriculum, such as in mathematics, where students learn to describe in words how they think about their own thinking. In one scene, a group of fifth graders surrounds a smaller group of students in a "fishbowl," watching, listening, and taking notes as the smaller group works on a problem of proportions with tiles. In a high school English class, students are asked to interview one another about their families and write essays, a project in which they learn about a classmate whose father has a drug problem or whose brother has a disability. District leaders point to the value of SEL across the curriculum, in math, English, and music, as reflected in the district's adequate yearly progress (AYP) on annual exams, where 39 of the 96 schools met AYP, and another 15 missed only 1 of 31 targets.

In Louisville, a district of more than 100,000 students, Superintendent Sheldon Berman arrived from the smaller district in Hudson, Massachusetts, which had achieved a reputation for creating a social/emotional learning foundation for students' learning. Louisville's Care for Kids program for elementary schools includes morning meetings, where students and teachers meet in small advisories at the start of each day to check in personally with one another. A secret benefit of SEL programs is making teaching more enjoyable for teachers. With less time spent on discipline and punishment, and with students happier and more willing to learn, teachers are able to focus on why they entered the profession in the first place—to teach.

An important landmark study has validated the connection between implementation of SEL curricula and academic achievement. A meta-analysis of 213 studies of social/emotional curricula in K–12 schools found a positive and substantial connection with students' academic achievement.[3] On average, groups of students in SEL programs outperformed matched samples of those without such instruction by 11 percentile points, a larger and more consistent gain across many studies than for nearly all other educational interventions.

Some teachers faced with the prospect of incorporating SEL into their teaching may say, "I don't have time to teach another strategy. I can't add another program to an already full plate." Dr. Roger Weissberg, president of the Collaborative for Academic, Social, and Emotional Learning and an author of the meta-analysis, responds that "this isn't adding something to your plate. This *is* the plate." SEL programs are the platform, the foundation, on which all other learning is built. Unless children feel good about themselves as people and as learners, unless they're "ready to learn," they won't learn.

LEARNING BECOMES INTERNET-IONAL

Preparing American students to be global thinkers ranks high on lists of 21st-century skills. In the Framework for 21st Century Learning, published by the Partnership for 21st Century Skills, "global awareness" is described as one of five interdisciplinary themes, along with four other new "literacies"—financial and economic, civic, health, and environmental—that should be integrated across the traditional subject areas. The Framework defines the global "literacy" as "using 21st century skills to understand and address global issues; learning from and working collaboratively with individuals representing diverse cultures, religions, and lifestyles in a spirit of mutual respect and open dialogue in personal, work, and community contexts; and understanding other nations and cultures, including use of non-English languages"[4]

Today's students are enthusiastically embracing learning about the rest of the globe. Thanks to the Internet, they are accessing differing sources of knowledge from around the world, from BBC World News and Al Jazeera newscasts to chatting with their peers over Skype to share lifestyles and learn languages. With these international experiences, in person and online, earlier in their childhoods, they will be our first truly global generation. The Internet has made learning *Internet-ional*.

Starting in 2004, Edutopia created a partnership with the Asia Society to document some of the best American schools leading the way to students' global futures. Documentary films, articles, and two DVDs were produced to document schools such as:

- *Walter Payton College Prep High School* in Chicago. Students study one of five languages, including Chinese, for all 4 years. A distance-learning center enables live videoconferencing with students around the globe, such as in South Africa, and students participate in home stay exchanges. The school has the only Confucius Institute at a high school, typically placed at universities and funded by the Chinese Ministry of Education, to support learning of Chinese language and culture.
- *International School of the Americas*, San Antonio. The curriculum includes visits to local museums, trips to Mexico,

and competing in the Model United Nations. The Edutopia film showed how one enterprising teacher, confronted with the cost of buses for field trips, obtained her bus driver's license, thereby enabling her to use the city as her students' classroom.

- *The International Education and Resource Network's First People's Project.* Choctaw students in Mississippi sharing stories with indigenous students in Thailand and Australia through IEARN's First People's Project. Thanks to their teachers and tribal elders, students learn Choctaw stories, history, and sports, and share them through the Internet with the larger world. Upon learning of the impoverished circumstances of Thai students, they organized a drive to donate blankets to their Internet pen pals.

- *K–12 Japanese Magnet Program,* Portland, Oregon. This Japanese immersion program is based on research that young children's brains are wired for language learning and that second-language learning may encourage cognitive development. In 5th grade, students compose email using Japanese word processors, host Japanese students, and visit them near Tokyo. Eighth graders go to Japan for a 2-week residency to complete an interdisciplinary project.

- *High Tech High,* San Diego. Students learned DNA testing procedures on meat samples to confirm poached meat in African markets. They and their teacher traveled to Tanzania to hold a workshop for local game officials on the identification of bushmeat. Team teaching between humanities and science teachers is common, such as in the Waterways to Peace project, where study of African politics related to the scarcity of water led to creating a model plant for water purification.

DOCUMENTING RESEARCH OUTCOMES
OF INNOVATIVE PRACTICES

While our work at edutopia.org has spanned more than 15 years of telling the stories of project-based learning and cooperative learning in classrooms, as well as in informal and after-school settings, we understood that for these "islands of excellence" to scale to more places, their effectiveness must be demonstrated in educational research. Importantly, policymakers investing funds in these new curricula, technology, and teacher development want to base their decisions on documented outcomes.

Our Foundation supported Dr. Linda Darling-Hammond and colleagues at Stanford University and the University of California, Berkeley, to review the literature on practices such as project-based learning, cooperative learning, and specific instructional strategies in literacy, mathematics, and science.[5] Their analyses took advantage of important new developments in cognitive research, such as the landmark 1999 volume, *How People Learn*, published by the National Academy of Sciences. They identified high-quality studies of the effectiveness of these strategies, more numerous with cooperative learning than with project-based learning. They also underscored the most important finding of all: that the effect of these innovations relies heavily on the quality of the teachers—and the professional development provided to them—who have to implement new practices. They also called for investments in new forms of research designs and measures to study these practices.

LISTENING TO THE PUBLIC ABOUT PUBLIC EDUCATION

While the voices of governors, legislators, and national leaders of unions, school boards, and the business community often are heard loudly in debates about the future of our schools, we rarely hear from the public itself. For more than 40 years, Phi Delta Kappa, the education honorary society, has surveyed a cross-section of Americans about their opinions regarding public schools.[6]

This survey should be read by every elected official, school board member, journalist, and educator. The American public is resoundingly clear—consistently about 70%—in its convictions about the importance of teachers and giving them more "flexibility to teach in ways they think best." The public, using its own common sense, knows that teacher effectiveness is a stronger determinant of academic achievement than class size. However, close to 70% also say they see and hear more negative than positive press about education. We could improve our schools more quickly if we told ourselves more stories about our best teachers and students.

The public also believes that access to the Internet for education is now the civil rights issue of our time. With as near unanimity as our diverse public ever achieves, 91% believe that providing all students with access to the Internet is important. They see its benefits in leveling the playing field of course offerings for smaller and rural schools, improving students' motivation, and preparing them for college and career.

So, Superman has indeed arrived, in the form of an army of super-educators across the country and an intelligent public. Our collective job should be to spread the good news of the innovative classrooms in many communities and invest in better research on their modern forms of digital learning. Together, perhaps we can make this the first decade of the 21st century in education.

NOTES

1. P. Burness, ed., *Learn & Live* (San Rafael, CA: George Lucas Educational Foundation, 1997); M. Chen and S. Armstrong, eds., *Edutopia: Success Stories for Learning in the Digital Age* (San Francisco: Jossey-Bass, 2003); M. Chen, *Education Nation: Six Leading Edges of Innovation in Our Schools* (San Francisco: Jossey-Bass, 2010).

2. P. Tough, "What If the Secret to Success Is Failure?" *New York Times Magazine*, http://www.nytimes.com/2011/09/18/magazine/what-if-the-secret-to-success-is-failure.html?pagewanted=all (September 14, 2011).

3. J. Durlak, R. Weissberg, A. Dymnicki, R. Taylor, and K. Schellinger, "The Impact of Enhancing Students' Social and Emotional Learning: A Meta-Analysis of School-Based Universal Interventions," *Child Development* 82, no. 1 (2011): 405–32.

4. See http://www.p21.org/overview/skills-framework/256.

5. L. Darling-Hammond, B. Barron, D. Pearson, A. Schoenfeld, E. Stage et al., *Powerful Learning: What We Know About Teaching for Understanding* (San Francisco: Jossey-Bass, 2007).

6. W. Bushaw and S. Lopez, "Betting on Teachers: The 43rd Annual Phi Delta Kappa/Gallup Poll of the Public's Attitudes Toward the Public Schools," *Phi Delta Kappan* 93, no. 1 (2011, September): 8–26.

CHAPTER 6

Waiting for Superman
with Clark Kent

Daniel A. Domenech

The perception that education in America is failing is wrong. The reality is that education in America is the best that it has ever been. As a matter of fact, the American education system can now boast of having the best performance benchmarks ever. According to the National Center for Education Statistics' *Trends in High School Dropout and Completion Rates in the United States: 1972–2008*, we now have the highest number of high school graduates in the history of our country. And it is not just a matter of an increasing population; the completion rate, at 89.9%, is the highest ever. Conversely, we have the lowest dropout rate ever, 3.5%, and since 1972 the number of dropouts has decreased by 60%.

Every June thousands of high school students graduate with honors, with advanced placement courses and international baccalaureate certificates, with earned college credits, and with acceptance into the best institutions of higher education in the world. There are twice as many students taking advanced placement courses now than there were 10 years ago, and the number of students enrolling in institutions of higher education has been increasing steadily. Across the country, school systems abound where more than 90% of students graduate from high school and more than 80% of the graduates go on to further their education.

In "America's High School Graduates: Results from the 2009 NAEP High School Transcript Study," the results show that today's graduates earn more credits and complete higher curriculum levels. In 2009, graduates earned over three credits more than their 1990 counterparts, or about 400 additional hours of instruction during their high school careers. And in 2009, a greater percentage of graduates than in 1990 or 2005 completed higher curriculum levels with greater course requirements. The NAEP scores in 4th- and 8th-grade reading and math are also the highest that they have ever been.

WAITING FOR "SUPERMAN": USING THE WRONG LENS TO VIEW PUBLIC EDUCATION

The movie *Waiting for "Superman"* depicts an education system that is not representative of public education in America. It is representative of the poor quality of education that too many of our language minority children and children of poverty receive in some rural and urban settings. Those are the schools where children are being left behind—and shame on America for letting it happen. But those are not the majority of schools in America. They are the 5% lowest performing schools. They include the dropout factories that house large percentages of minority children and children of poverty.

The problem with *Waiting for "Superman"* is that it paints all of public education with a single brush. It creates the erroneous public perception that all of our schools are failing, when that is clearly not the case. This has led a host of education "reformers" to push for the same solutions for all schools, when those solutions might be appropriate primarily for the failing schools. The parents with children in functioning schools are not looking for choice, vouchers, or charters. They are not looking to have the principal and half of the teaching staff replaced. They are pleased with the education their child is receiving. The most recent Phi Delta Kappa/Gallup Poll tells us that 75% of parents in this country assign a grade of A or B to the school attended by their oldest child. That is the highest percentage ever recorded in response to that question.

Undoubtedly, in spite of our education system now being the best
that it has ever been, we want it to be better. Americans have never
been happy with the status quo. We are constantly attempting to
improve all facets of our lives. However, saying that we want our
schools to be better is much different from saying that all of our
schools are failing. The latter has led to the supposition that our
current crop of educators is part of the problem, rather than being
part of the solution. That is also incorrect. People are waiting for
Superman when Clark Kent is already in their midst. Our schools are
now the best they have ever been because our teachers and principals
and administrators are the products of those schools and consequently
are better trained than their predecessors.

Not all minority children and children of poverty attend schools
like the ones depicted in the movie. Many, with the identical
demographic background, attend traditional schools where they
thrive and receive an excellent education. It is not as if our teachers
and administrators are at a loss as to what to do for these children.
They do know what works, and successful examples abound in
communities throughout America. Two of the top-rated school
systems in the nation, Montgomery County in Maryland and Fairfax
County in Virginia, have demographic profiles and diversity matching
those of the nation. Yet both districts are acknowledged for providing
quality education to students like the ones depicted in *Waiting for
"Superman."*

WHAT WE CAN DO TO IMPROVE OUR PUBLIC SCHOOLS

America's schools are the best they have ever been, but what can
we do to make them better? We certainly can learn from what our
successful school systems are doing. There are also many legitimate
"reform" efforts that are on the right track to transforming our failing
schools. The personification of the Superman the movie refers to is
Geoffrey Canada, recently named to *Time* magazine's list of the most
influential people in the world. As president and CEO of New York's
Harlem Children's Zone, Canada created a program that has become

the prime example of how charters can provide at-risk children with the education and support that will allow them to prosper in an otherwise bleak environment. Indeed, the Harlem Children's Zone became the model for President Obama's federally funded Promise Neighborhood Initiative.

Canada is all about providing children from impoverished communities with the services and support that they will need to survive and thrive. In communities like Harlem, schools must take on broader responsibilities than just teaching a child to read and write. All of the factors external to the classroom that affect learning are taken into consideration and coordinated with instructional activities. The Harlem Children's Zone is about the education of the total child.

Dysfunctional schools cannot do it alone, and community support and services for the children must be coordinated to provide for the total needs of the child. Communities in Schools (CIS) is a national not-for-profit organization that leverages available community services and support to provide for the needs of students. CIS works within the public school system to determine student needs and establish relationships with local businesses, social service agencies, health care providers, and parent and volunteer organizations to provide needed resources. Serving over 1.3 million students across the nation, CIS has achieved an impressive record in helping students stay in school and graduate.

America's Promise Alliance's Grad Nation campaign is yet another effort that is attempting to harness the willingness of the corporate sector, foundations, and community agencies to help schools through the delivery of needed services to students. The success of these efforts is often dependent on the degree of cooperation and collaboration between the outside agencies and the school. In the Harlem Children's Zone the services are built into the organization that Canada has created. CIS provides a coordinator who works in the school and frees the school staff to focus on what they do best, teach. When the services are not part of the program or coordinated by someone outside of the school, issues of turf, privacy, and accountability can emerge and school personnel may put up walls to keep the well-intentioned service providers out, resulting in a waste of precious resources.

One of the more successful charter school networks is the Knowledge Is Power Program. There are currently 99 KIPP schools in 20 states and the District of Columbia serving more than 27,000 students. More than 80% of the students are from low-income families and 95% are either African American or Hispanic. As with the Harlem Children's Zone, KIPP also boasts impressive results with a population of students usually associated with failure. The current charter school controversy pits charter schools against traditional schools. In *"Superman"* the traditional schools were the problem, and charter schools were billed as the solution. In fact, charter schools today instruct only 3% of our student population. The Stanford University CREDO study on charter schools shows wide variation in performance. The study reveals that a decent fraction of charter schools—17%—provide superior educational opportunities for their students. Nearly half of the charter schools nationwide have results that are no different from the local public school options, and over a third—37%—deliver learning results that are significantly worse than their students would have realized had they remained in traditional public schools. With only a 17% chance of improving on the performance of traditional schools, charter schools are an option but certainly not *the* solution.

THE IMPACT OF POVERTY ON ACADEMIC ACHIEVEMENT AND OPPORTUNITY

The evidence strongly suggests that poverty is the factor that seems to have the highest correlation with student achievement. When NAEP results are correlated with the percentage of students in a school receiving free or reduced lunch, we obtain almost a perfect negative correlation. The higher the percentage of students on free and reduced lunch, the lower the academic performance. Conversely, poor students in schools with a low percentage of poverty perform significantly better than their counterparts in a highly impacted school. The same is true for students who are not on free and reduced lunch. Their performance is adversely affected if they attend a school with a high percentage of children receiving lunch aid.

The programs that we have highlighted thus far confront the poverty issue and attempt to neutralize it by providing students with the support structure that they lack because of their impoverished background. Proper nutrition, health services, and child care are needs that must be tended to before the educational needs of the child can be met. We also understand that the achievement gap develops long before children reach school. Several NAEP reports have revealed that while first-time kindergartners are similar in many ways, their knowledge and skills differ in relation to their age at school entry, race/ethnicity, health status, home educational experiences, and child care histories. Preschool programs that expose children of poverty to experiences that nonpoverty children have had prior to school entry will help to level the playing field.

The conditions that create the deficit for poor children prior to entry in school do not disappear once they are in school. Extended learning opportunities must be maintained during the school year. This model is a critical component of the KIPP success story. KIPP schools have an extended learning day that typically runs from 7:30 a.m. to 5:00 p.m., with a biweekly half-day Saturday program. The school year is also 2 weeks longer than the traditional school year, averaging 192 days.

Traditional educators are envious of KIPP's ability to provide so much additional time for learning. If school districts attempted to replicate the KIPP model, however, they would experience significant budget increases that would meet taxpayer opposition. Yet, if we are serious about closing the achievement gap, that is what we need to do to overcome the deficit poor children bring to school.

GETTING REAL ABOUT SCHOOL REFORM

Part of the problem is that we are not truly attempting to transform schools. Educational reform efforts in America are generally akin to rearranging the chairs on the deck of the Titanic. The charter schools that succeed do so because they can get waivers that allow them to get around the rules and regulations that the public schools have to adhere to. Charters also can attract money from corporations, foundations, and public donations, which provide them with greater resources than the public schools have.

But extending time on task is not a revolutionary idea. We have known forever that if you allow children more time to learn, they will learn more. The main obstacle has always been the finances. America's public school system cannot afford the additional 10 to 20% increases in operating expenses that extending the school day and the school year would cost. A more reasonable approach would be to extend the school day and the school year for just those children who need it. That, however, would create logistical problems, and both the parents of the children who would have to spend more time in school and the other parents, who would feel that their kids were being left out, would balk.

A truly transformational approach would eliminate the time factor as the fixed variable. We now require all students to be in school for the same number of hours and the same number of days. In addition, we require all students to acquire the same knowledge within the same period of time. The result is that about one third of all students are bored and distracted because the pace of instruction is not keeping up with their intellectual abilities. For another third of the students, the pace is just right. But for the final third of the students, the learning time is not enough and the pace of instruction is too fast for them to keep up. These are the students that fall behind and eventually drop out of school.

Imagine instead a system where knowledge acquisition became the variable rather than time. Our nation is in pursuit of the adoption of common core standards. Ideally the day will come when all 50 states will agree on what every child should know and tests will have been developed to ascertain that knowledge. Simultaneous with the adoption of the common core standards could be a shift away from time (e.g., every student must know X by the end of first grade, and so on, through high school graduation) to competency-based instruction, where students will have whatever time they need to master a body of knowledge before they are allowed to move on to the next level of work. Under this framework, students would be learning at an individualized pace of instruction. Some students would not need 13 years of schooling. They could graduate and go on to college much sooner. Others might require 14, 15, or even 16 years, but they would leave with the same body of knowledge and ready for college or career.

This would be a major paradigm shift that would require us to abandon the current K–12 grade-level structure and replace it with something more akin to the number of credits accumulated at the college level. However, it is doable and would not incur the prohibitive costs of extending the school year and the school day. We are wed to an organizational structure for our schools that is the root of most of the problems we face in our attempts to educate every child and leave no child behind. Moving away from the current grade levels and time requirements and establishing a model based on knowledge acquisition through an individualized learning pace would be a real step toward 21st-century schooling.

IMPROVING TEACHER QUALITY

In addition to poverty and how our schools are structured, another significant factor affecting how children learn is the quality of the instruction. Teacher quality is widely recognized as the most essential in-school factor affecting student learning, but here again attempts at reform have not been truly transformational. The current approach is to evaluate and fire our way to improved teacher quality. Paralleling the misconception that all children should learn the same material at the same time, is the notion that once teachers graduate from college and are hired, they will need no ongoing professional development or support. We need a continuous improvement model similar to what the most successful countries in the world use to develop and sustain a highly trained and well-supported educator workforce.

The role of the teacher is rapidly changing. The teacher as the talking head in the front of the classroom, the sage on the stage, belongs with vinyl records, the rotary phone, and the overhead projector. Today's teacher needs to be more a director of learning and less the person in the front of the room delivering a lecture.

Technology can facilitate this new teacher role, with online learning allowing for more individualized instruction, formative assessment, and classroom management. But the integration of technology into learning activities requires ongoing professional development so that teachers can keep up with a rapidly changing field. Within a few years we have gone from desktop computers to laptops and now handheld devices. Keeping up with the hardware, software, and the growing list of products is a herculean task.

Education system leaders understand the need for ongoing professional development but, historically, professional development is one of the last activities to be budgeted and one of the first to be cut during hard economic times. The impact of the current economic recession has taken a drastic toll on professional development activities in school systems throughout the country. Current reform efforts focus on the removal of inept teachers from the classroom but not on the development and retention of existing teachers. Many are targeting the teacher unions as the culprits in protecting incompetent individuals and allowing them to remain in the classroom. The solution here is better labor–management collaboration. Management must agree to provide the support and development structure that will give all of our teachers the opportunity to become the best teachers they can be. At the same time labor must abandon the protection of incompetent teachers and support their dismissal when development opportunities have been provided and the teachers are still unable to function effectively. The American Association of School Administrators (AASA) and the American Federation of Teachers have collaborated on the development of a framework that would accomplish both goals.

CONCLUSION: EDUCATING THE WHOLE CHILD

In summary, in spite of current attacks on our public education system, America's public schools are the best they have ever been. We want them to be better, particularly the bottom 5% that are failing our minority, second-language-learner, and impoverished students. To succeed we need to educate the total child by bringing into the classroom all of the support elements the community can provide. We also need to change the current structure that expects all children to learn the same thing in the same amount of time. Let's establish specific outcomes for what children should know, but allow them the time they need to learn it. We also need to focus on teacher quality by providing teachers with ongoing development and support. That is how we can make all of America's schools better.

CHAPTER 7

Superman Isn't Coming (at Least Not with the Red Cape and the Phone Booth)

Peter Smith

Viewing *Waiting for "Superman"* reawakened long-dormant experiences and instincts that have been buried in me for many years. For instance:

- I believe in a diverse set of school models, including charter schools.
- I believe that gifted teachers and leaders make a huge difference in the quality of what happens in school.
- I know that parents and the education level of parents are important.
- I know that money matters. People who have it get more money for their schools and their children do better in school. And people who don't have it get less money for their schools and their children do less well in school.
- I don't believe in identified "devils" (the unions) or silver bullets (magnet schools). If this problem were simple to solve, we would have done so over the past 40 years.
- And I believe that we have the tools for solutions to our learning and school problems emerging in the web 2.0 world,

if we choose to employ them to change the fundamental teaching–learning model.

When I first attended graduate school in education, I was greeted by a volley of books brimming with rage at the failure of the public education system to serve all children, especially poor children and children of color, equally and well. They had powerful titles and carried hot messages—*Death At an Early Age, How Children Fail, The Little Red Schoolhouse, Village School Downtown*—and they furnished the narrative line that drove innovation following passage of the Civil Rights Act of 1964. Along with these publications came a movie, *High School*, by Frederic Wiseman. It was a visual chronicle of the deadly boredom and hopelessness that filled one American high school like a miasmic fog.

Waiting for "Superman" is of that genre: downright "angrifying," to quote former baseball great Satchel Paige. Watching eager children and their parents as their future is decided by a lottery made me sick at heart. How is it possible that, after all these years and with twice as much being spent on the enterprise in constant dollars today than we did then, we could have stalled so badly in our drive to successfully educate a significantly higher percentage of our children, especially poor children? And while the debate about academic quality rages, the data continue to indicate growing problems in that area as well. Not only are our completion rates still unacceptably low, but those who do graduate are no longer the best educated high school graduates in the world. And, according to one recent book, *Academically Adrift*,[1] high school graduates who actually make it to college use their time in predominantly nonacademic pursuits, learning less and playing more. Can it really be true that current college students, on average, spend less than 20% of their time studying and attending class?

We have failed to significantly increase the percentage of people completing high school and going to college. And we have failed to crack the barriers of income and race as gross impediments to success in the American education system.

This is not a small-stakes game. Our failure to turn our elementary and high schools into places of imagination, creativity, culture, and learning ultimately will, I believe, doom American democracy as we know, understand, and experience it. Education leads to a seat at the table of opportunity in America. Indeed, if the promise of opportunity—or a better life—is the lifeblood of our democracy, then a fully functioning and successful education system is its beating heart. At the risk of making a bad pun, let me suggest that participating in our democracy is an elective activity. People can choose to get into it or sit it out.

People with hope and opportunity will get in. But when democracy is not working for them, they will be inclined to sit it out—if they are not left out by a system that intends to exclude their participation. Education is the ticket to a life where the bearer lives longer and with greater health, earns more, and participates in civil society at greater rates, including politics. So, when someone asks me for the "data" on the return rendered by a good K–12 and postsecondary system, these are the data I use.

In the pages ahead, I will discuss some reasons why we have not been able to "move the needle" on student success and then will suggest some policies and actions that indicate what we might do to get the changes in K–12 education that we so desperately need. My purpose is not to have the "best" idea. Rather it is to open the door to, and encourage, different thinking about schools, schooling, and school reform.

FUNDING AND ACCOUNTABILITY

Over the past 40 years, I have had the honor of serving on my local school board in a small town in rural Vermont, working in the Vermont State Department of Education, serving in the Vermont State Senate on the Education Committee, and serving in the U.S. House of Representatives on the Education and Labor Committee. As a university president and a graduate education dean, I worked with local school districts and trained teachers for 15 years. And as Assistant Director General for Education at UNESCO in Paris, I worked with ministers of education around the world to craft solutions for elementary and secondary education problems as part of UNESCO's "Education for All" initiative. Along the way I served on several national panels and the boards of national policy groups, becoming fairly well grounded in both education and workforce policy and practice.

Based on what I have learned collectively from these experiences, *Waiting for "Superman"* correctly identifies one of the major reasons why so many schools are "dried out," so barren of success and hope, and so divorced from the intention of state and federal legislative policy. The fundamental problem has two dimensions:

1. National and state policies and regulations, coupled with multiple sources of funding, create an environment in which the intentions behind the policies and funding are sacrificed at the twin altars of bureaucratic regulation and poor accountability measures.
2. These two realities combine to put the interests of the child behind those of almost everyone else involved— teachers, bureaucrats, parents, and others. They are all well intentioned with the "best interests of the child" at heart, but come with agendas that, when satisfied, leave precious little for the children involved.

Put more simply, we lack national and state agendas that are premised on the fundamental truth that education happens on the ground, locally, between and among people.

FROM SCARCITY TO ABUNDANCE

The fundamental premise behind the "big" school movement was established in the 1950s by the former president of Harvard, James Bryant Conant. He asserted, without a lot of data, that 750 students were needed to generate sufficient resources for a quality education. That assertion, always questionable in some minds, has been flipped upside down by information technology and the web.

Our schools are organized around the assumption of scarcity. There is not enough organized knowledge, so we collect it in one place and plan a curriculum based on a set of textbooks. There are not enough books, so we develop and populate a library with books and periodicals. There is nowhere to practice chemistry, so we build a lab. There are not enough experts, so we train teachers and put them in front of kids.

All these practices, and many others that spring from the concept of scarcity, may have been the answer prior to 1990. Since then, however, we have been living in an age of increasing information abundance, cognitive science, open education resources, e-labs, and links to curricula and experts of all kinds, as well as diagnostic and advising services that outstrip what any guidance counselor can know and do. Now, when we can touch the world through the web while sitting in a school in rural South Dakota or downtown Phoenix, a locally derived education does not have to mean a limited education. The education world has become as flat as Thomas Friedman's economic and communications world.

In this emerging ecology of abundance, however, our schools remain little silos sitting at the bottom of an enormous education hierarchy. We persist in trying to solve the problems from the top down, using the old hierarchy required by scarcity.

Here is a case in point. As I sat in the Congress, I watched the rule-making process at the Department of Education take broadly crafted legislation and narrow its intent before sending it on to the states. And I watched states further narrow the intention to ensure "accountability" at the district level. This cascade of narrowing intentions proceeded apace at the district level because no one wanted trouble with the state and the feds. And so, time after time, the intent of legislation that was as vast as the Great Plains when passed in Washington, more resembled Rhode Island when it got to where the action really was: teachers, the classroom, and kids.

This narrowing of interpretation, and the resulting multifaceted bureaucratic straitjacketing of local districts, teachers, principals, and parents, reveals one of the fundamental principles we must establish if we want schools to improve. We need to separate school accountability from the sources of funding, while incentivizing completion and better assessment of learning. And we need to be more concerned about the results than the model that achieves them.

As I look across the emerging policy recommendations, ranging from the "common core" (for curriculum), to alternative assessments that can change schools from teaching factories to places of learning, to better and more nimble career- and college-advising services, I see the most robust conversation occurring within and among the states, driven by groups like the National Governors Association, the Council of Chief State School Officers, and the Council for State Governments, as well as major foundations. In part, this conversation has been enabled and fueled by the emergence of the web and social networking as powerful influencers in the K–12 arena. Information and data, as well as curricula and assessments, can be shared and used to improve learning in ways that were unimaginable even 10 years ago.

Focusing on outcomes that are interpreted and enabled at the state and local level is an approach far superior to a strong federal regulatory hand. Regardless of the money it puts on the table, the U.S. Department of Education must discipline itself to be a source of money and ideas, while resisting the temptation to use its financial clout to enforce a federal worldview. If we learned anything from No Child Left Behind, it was about the shallowness of high-stakes testing and the aridity of a national discussion, enforced by law, about one way of saving the schools.

DIMINISHING RETURNS?

Waiting for "Superman" makes another important point: We need to look at how we deploy the money, time, and talent that we have in play before we cry for more. It just may be that the existing model is "maxed out," exemplifying the law of diminishing returns. Any model has limitations to its productivity and, hence, success. If the traditional model is working at its capacity, we need additional, new models, not just more money. For example, it turns out that Washington, DC, and other poorly functioning districts, spend a lot of money on education. It's just that the kids don't see it.

When I served as dean of the Graduate School of Education and Human Development at George Washington University 20 years ago, I discovered two things: First, more than 50 cents of every dollar spent in the district fell outside of the schools themselves. Less than half the money appropriated actually got to the schools! Second, if I wanted to reach the superintendent of the DC schools, Dr. Franklin Smith, I had to call him at home because I couldn't get through at the office.

Michelle Rhee's experience suggests that both of these circumstances still existed when she became superintendent more than 15 years later. Furthermore, her experience also underscores the stark and unyielding reality that the effort to bring new models, in Washington or anywhere else, still faces the uphill battle against an entrenched culture that, however well intentioned, is not succeeding in the one job that matters: successfully educating children.

We need new concepts, for governance and for schools, that recognize the local nature of the educational enterprise while avoiding the head-to-head battles that so often characterize, and doom, education reform efforts. What might these new concepts look like? Some might be "sustaining innovations," extending and improving the traditional model, along the lines of Clayton Christensen's thinking in *The Innovator's Dilemma*:[2]

- Can we give local schools the support they need to innovate in ways that make sense to them: merit pay in one place, high-stakes testing or reflective assessment and blended learning in another?
- Can we create legislative and policy "space" that puts districts and teachers in the driver's seat instead of the caboose?
- Can we craft an accountable "creative decentralization" policy that asks each district to stipulate its goals, and the means to achieve them, and hold them accountable?
- If we can have charter schools, why can't we have charter districts?

- Can we teach content at home and do homework, exercise, art, music, and reflection at school, reversing the uses of time?
- Can we extend the role of the teacher to include "supporter of learning" when the "teacher as content expert" is not available?

For example, the proposal discussed in *Waiting for "Superman"* to layer in merit pay as a choice for teachers was simple and smart. It also would have allowed for the development of metrics and comparisons that would have put the combative arguments between unions and merit pay advocates to rest with real data.

In the creative and accountable decentralization that I see, I would want to give the high-stakes testing that has paralyzed so many teachers and students across the country some company—other forms of assessment such as reflective assessment using portfolios, where teachers and students actually produce work and discuss it. Some districts may want to graduate students who can remember and regurgitate, the memorizers. And if they do, so be it. But an increasing number of colleges and employers want thinkers, people who can adapt to new situations, work on teams, and bring abstract thought down to the ground. Let me give an example.

A friend of mine sits on the Vermont State Board of Education. He recently was asked and agreed to serve as a judge for the state spelling bee finals. As a writer and communications professional, he thought it would be interesting. Shortly after the event, he called me in disbelief. "Peter," he said, "you won't believe what happened. We went through four rounds and very few contestants were eliminated. It was astonishing; they were spelling words correctly that I have never heard of. Then, when we had run through the source books, the organizers had to come up with other words. They were far simpler. But the kids started falling like flies, misspelling very simple words that any high school junior should know. I could not believe it!"

What is the explanation for kids being able to spell difficult words, but not simple words? As he probed for an answer, he was told that the kids had studied (i.e., memorized) the source books. As a consequence, they knew those words by heart. But when they had to actually sound a word out and spell it from scratch, they were far less adept.

Different people have different views on testing, how to do it best, what they want as a result, what is most effective. As we develop a deeper appreciation of learning outcomes, why not let school districts and states decide how they want to address assessment and evaluation issues? If we developed this type of approach, it would allow every district in America to solve the problem of declining student learning, especially for poorer students, in a way that made sense to it and for which it would be accountable. Here's another example of how two districts or regions can differ enormously.

When I was Assistant Director General for Education at UNESCO, the agency did a study on teacher availability in sub-Saharan Africa. In general terms, it found that if all the teacher-training programs performed at full effectiveness, there would be fewer teachers per child in 2016 than there were when the study was completed in 2006. There were a variety of contributing factors. But the one that stood out for me was that a trained teacher was a hotter economic commodity than a person without the certificate or degree. The trained teacher had lots of job options, many of which lay outside of education. In other words, people could leave teaching and make more money.

Does that sound familiar? Whether you are in rural New Mexico or urban LA, Lagos or Mumbai, the problem is the same. We do not pay teachers enough to keep them, especially the extremely talented ones, in the practice. The persistent leaving of the profession consistently undermines our capacity to succeed. And the turnover is far worse in poorer school districts and geographic regions.

For example, in California, where more first-year teachers are graduated every year than in any other state in America, 15–18% of all classrooms routinely are populated by teachers without a teaching credential. And when you look at these data and cut them by hard-to-teach and hard-to-learn subjects, the numbers skyrocket. Also, understandably, it is a worse problem in poor districts than in those with additional resources.

So, while understanding that the situations in California or rural New Mexico are far different than in Lagos or Mumbai, they share a common problem that has not been solved: not enough trained and persisting teachers. Having seen this problem in both California and Africa, and realizing that it is a problem that has resisted solution throughout my career, I framed a different way of stating it.

Instead of simply calling for more and better trained and paid teachers (for which, unfortunately, there appears to be little or no appetite), let's ask a different question. How can children learn successfully *without* the necessary ratio of trained teachers?

- Can we use technology to create consistent and high-quality content, backed up by experts, both in the school and on the web?
- Can we train high-quality learning support staff who can support the learner and the learning, providing the human dimension that is necessary for reflection and learning?
- Can we rethink the use of time both at home and in school to increase its effective impact on learning?

CONCLUSION

There is no simple solution to these problems, and one chapter in a book cannot possibly elaborate even one complex solution. My intent is a different one: to open the door to new thinking.

Today, we know how to create high-quality, highly adaptive curricula with great built-in diagnostics for all grade levels. They would bring consistency, validity, and reliability to the interplay between teaching, learning, and assessment. The science and the technology are there.

And we can create environments where learners are practicing, reflecting, and learning with the help of trained staff. If content and assessment can be brought in adaptive, compelling, and excellent ways to the learning experience, why wouldn't we consider a different use of the learners' and the teachers' time; a use that focused on learning and support, rather than "standing and delivering" on the one hand and "sitting and listening" on the other.

Agreeing on learning outcomes and having a tested variety of ways of assessing those outcomes would allow for local variety while ensuring consistency. I, for one, cannot believe that a one-size-fits-all approach aligns well with the diversity that is America or with our tradition of federalism. Asking schools to set their standards and then holding them accountable for meeting those standards would seem to be a better way to go.

Finally, can we imagine additional types of professionals in schools who are learning specialists, not just subject matter specialists? With that kind of adaptation, we could maximize the value of the technology and web-based materials, while supporting the learners and their learning locally.

Superman is on the way, but he doesn't have a red cape and he won't stop the runaway school bus with one hand. That's the bad news. The good news is that this Superman is turbo-charged by web 2.0, social networking, rich resources, and highly consistent academic quality. Also, this Superman does not need to do it all himself. He likes to share the capacity to save people.

NOTES

1. R. Arum and J. Roksa, *Academically Adrift: Limited Learning on College Campuses* (Chicago: Univerisity of Chicago Press, 2011).
2. C. Christensen, *The Innovator's Dilemma: The Revolutionary Book That Will Change the Way You Do Business* (New York: HarperBusiness, 2000).

CHAPTER 8

Whose Side Is Superman on, Anyway?

John Merrow

"Microfiche?" the 14-year-old asked, staring at the machines tucked away in the New York Public Library. "What's microfiche?"

How many people under age 30 could explain it? Her question is a powerful reminder of how technology has turned learning on its head. Just a few years ago, libraries and schools were the places that stored knowledge—on microfiche, in the *Encyclopedia Britannica*, and in the heads of the adults in charge. We had to go there to gain access to that knowledge.

Not any longer. Today knowledge and information are everywhere, 24/7, thanks to the Internet. Unless libraries have been closed because of budget cuts, they have adapted to this new world. Most have become multipurpose centers with Internet access that distribute books, audio books, and DVDs. Librarians encourage patrons to ask questions, because they need to keep the public coming through their doors.

By contrast, schools remain a monopoly, places where children are expected to answer questions, by filling in the bubbles or blanks and by speaking up when called upon. I call them "answer factories." Providing access to knowledge, one of three historical justifications for schools, no longer applies in the usual sense. Of course, children need teachers to help them learn to read and master numbers, but, beyond that, a new approach is required. (More about that later.)

A second justification, socialization, also has been turned on its head by technology. Today's kids don't need school for socialization in the usual sense of learning to get along with their peers in the building. Why? Because there are online places for that, dozens of them, including Facebook, FarmVille, and so on, and so "socialization" takes on new meanings when kids routinely text with "friends they've never met" across the continent or an ocean. Again, schools must adapt to this new reality.

Only custodial care, the third historical justification for school, remains unchanged. Parents still need places to send their children to keep them safe. So does the larger society, which has rejected child labor and does not want kids on the streets.

But when schools provide only custodial care and a marginal education that denies technology's reach and power, young people walk away, as at least 6,000 do every school day, for an annual dropout total of over 1 million.

And some of those who remain in marginal schools will find themselves in danger, because the youthful energy that ought to be devoted to meaningful learning inevitably will be released, somewhere. Often it comes out in bullying, cyber-bullying, and other forms of child abuse by children. That is, marginal education often produces dangerous schools.

Unfortunately, those in charge of public education have not been paying attention to these seismic changes. Instead they are warring over teacher competence, test scores, merit pay, and union rules, issues that are fundamentally irrelevant to the world children live in.

WHO ARE THESE WARRIORS?

On one side in this battle is a cadre of prominent superintendents and wealthy hedge fund managers. Led by former New York Schools Chancellor Joel Klein and former DC Chancellor Michelle Rhee, 15 leading school superintendents issued a 1,379-word manifesto in October 2010 asserting that the difficulty of removing incompetent teachers "has left our school districts impotent and, worse, has robbed millions of children of a real future."

This side believes in charter schools, Teach for America, and paying teachers based on their students' test scores. Publicly pushing this "free market" line is a powerful trio: Davis Guggenheim's *Waiting for "Superman"* movie; NBC's semi-journalistic exercise, Education Nation; and Oprah Winfrey. And if one movie isn't enough, this side also has *The Lottery* in the wings.

It has identified the villains: bad teachers and the evil unions that protect them, particularly Randi Weingarten of the American Federation of Teachers. Their solution: get rid of bad teachers and replace them with *Better People*. Many in the *Better People* group believe that smarter and more dedicated teachers are more likely to come from Teach for America (TFA) than from traditional schools of education. The *Better People* camp has established beachheads in New Orleans and Washington, DC, among other places. In New Orleans' Recovery School District (RSD), about half of the teachers are members of Teach for America, teaching at least one of every three students there, according to Wendy Kopp, the founder of TFA. TeachNOLA, a local version of TFA, has sent more than 400 teachers to the RSD since 2007. It's a rare school in New Orleans that doesn't have at least one teacher from TFA and TeachNOLA, and many have half a dozen or more teachers.

When she was chancellor in Washington, DC, Michelle Rhee eagerly recruited from TFA, not surprisingly, since she got her start in education with TFA. When Rhee took the job in 2007, her mentor Joel Klein gave her direct advice, "You have to get rid of people." And she did, firing or replacing several hundred teachers and over half of her principals.

Rhee's director of personnel told the *NewsHour* program that at least 50%—and perhaps as much as 80%—of the Washington teaching corps had neither the skill nor the motivation to succeed. On one level, that's an odd criticism, because isn't it the job of leadership—Rhee and her team, including her director of personnel—to provide motivation? Or is criticizing them for lack of motivation supposed to act as a motivator?

WAITING FOR "SUPERMAN"—THE MOVIE

As for *Waiting for "Superman"* itself, there's much to admire. Guggenheim and his colleagues know how to tell a story, the graphics are sensational, and some of the characters—notably Geoffrey Canada and the children—just jump off the screen. That said, the film strikes me as a mishmash of contradictions and unsupportable generalizations, even half-truths. Its message is oversimplified to the point of being insulting, which made its disappointing performance at the box office welcome news.

Some reviewers loved it (Tom Friedman and David Brooks in *The New York Times*; Barack Obama), but the message of the movie can be reduced to a couple of aphorisms: Charter schools are good, unions are bad, and great teachers are good.

Take the last point, one that no one can disagree with. Unfortunately, *Waiting for "Superman"* never takes the time to explore what makes a teacher great. As noted, the movie demonizes Weingarten and her union, the American Federation of Teachers, without giving her much of an opportunity to defend herself. Left off the hook completely are school boards (which signed and approved all those contracts!) and the National Education Association (NEA), the larger union and one that is more deeply entrenched in defending the status quo.

Charter schools are another confusing topic in the movie. Although there's a throwaway line that says something to the effect that only one out of five charter schools is outstanding, the message of the movie is that charter schools represent education's salvation. If only a small percentage of charters are great, shouldn't we find out what makes the great ones great (besides "great teachers," whatever they are)? If you missed that one line—and I suspect most in the audience did—then the message is simply wrong. Is that intentional, or merely careless, on the part of Guggenheim and his colleagues?

A significant contradiction involves the film's star, Geoffrey Canada. His intelligence, energy, and commitment simply jump off the screen, and he gets more "face time" than anyone else (or so it would seem—I didn't clock it). But Canada's prescription for saving youngsters is radical and very expensive—the Harlem Children's

Zone and services for children from birth and for their parents—and the movie pointedly does not endorse that approach. That makes no sense, and it seems to me that the moviemakers are capitalizing on Canada's charisma to advance their own feel-good agenda of great teachers, weak unions, and charter schools.

Michelle Rhee also is featured in the film, but unfortunately the material about her was already very much out of date when the movie was released. She comes across as surprisingly flat, which is odd given that she is as compelling a figure as Canada. In fact, the best moments with Rhee are those from our *NewsHour* series (which Guggenheim used over our strenuous objections).

The children are appealing, as are their parents, and their stories—trying to get into decent schools—are heartwrenching. I won't spoil the ending by revealing the results of the various lotteries, but I can't help but wonder about the "too good to be true" ending. As my dad used to say, "If something seems too good to be true, it probably is." (It later came out that Guggenheim staged scenes, an absolute no-no in the world of documentary films.)

The most revealing moment in the film is the graphic meant to depict teaching and learning: A child's skull is opened up, and an adult pours "information" into it. That says everything anyone needs to know about the filmmakers' grasp of education—they don't understand that deep learning involves a journey of discovery, or that true education is more a drawing out than a pouring in.

While President Obama has been urging greater respect for teachers (by pointing out that in South Korea teachers are known as "nation builders"), the attacks on the profession have only grown more intense since *Waiting for "Superman"* appeared. Politicians in Wisconsin, Ohio, New Jersey, and elsewhere regularly trash teachers, labeling them as greedy, overpaid, and lazy. Fox News is, no surprise, filling its air with attacks. In response, Jon Stewart on *The Daily Show* has been simply brilliant, skewering the hypocrisy of Fox and the politicians.

Of course, this is not a laughing matter. Who can calculate the damage being done to an honorable profession? Who benefits from this trashing? How many prospective teachers are now deciding on different careers because of what they are reading and hearing every day?

THE *BETTER JOB* VIEW

The competing *Better Job* view holds that the problem is with the job itself: Teachers aren't respected, classes are too large, administrators don't punish unruly students, and so forth. Therefore, the solution is to make teaching prestigious, rewarding, and attractive—a job worth fighting for. "Give teachers a clear set of outcomes and expectations, the tools they need, decent working conditions, and the time and trust that other professionals take for granted," the logic goes. That approach will solve most of education's problems.

Some evidence supports this view. Because teaching doesn't offer much prestige, authority, or pay, upward of 40% leave teaching within 5 years.

While the argument about professionalism may sound compelling, it's mostly talk. Contracts negotiated by unions and school boards provide an operational definition of *Better Job*. It generally means higher pay, a shorter day, smaller classes, and a quicker path to tenure. Some contracts allow teachers to arrive a few minutes before school starts and leave a few minutes after the closing bell. Contracts may sharply limit the number of faculty meetings or require that teachers give their permission before the principal may enter the classroom. This narrow, trade union definition obviously favors teachers, but it's difficult to see how it benefits students—or elevates the teaching profession.

In the battle against the *Better People* faction, the other side is clearly outnumbered: the NEA, the American Federation of Teachers, many teachers, and some Democrats. Its villains are No Child Left Behind and its narrow focus on bubble test scores in reading and math. This side's far weaker megaphone is wielded by historian Diane Ravitch, a former Bush education policymaker turned apostate. Ravitch has been particularly critical of Bill Gates and Eli Broad, whom she refers to as "the billionaire boys club."

Ironically, the two billionaires have been supporting both sides. Each, through his foundation, put money behind Guggenheim's movie and the first Education Nation, NBC's 3-day meeting in October 2010 that essentially echoed the free-market line about charter schools and bad unions. However, the Gates Foundation also is spending millions to promote union–school board collaboration in Hillsborough, Florida, and elsewhere. As for Broad, it spends millions training school leaders; what's more, the 2010 prestigious Broad Prize in Urban Education went to a school district that is being sued by its state for refusing to allow charter schools.

In Washington, the *Better People* argument seems to be winning. Race to the Top language rarely refers to making teaching a more desirable occupation. Secretary of Education Arne Duncan, a supporter of Teach for America when he led Chicago's schools, has endorsed alternative teacher-training pathways and criticized schools of education for low standards. He and the President support linking teacher pay and student performance, and the Department of Education is encouraging testing in areas beyond language arts, math, and science.

Both sides ignore reality. The free-market crowd's enthusiasm for charter schools sidesteps data showing that only 17% of the country's 5,000 charter schools outperform their public counterparts, while 37% significantly underperform comparable public schools. (The likely explanation for the range of quality of charter schools is the quality of the charter, the original contract; where standards are high, charter schools seem to do well, while in places like Texas and Arizona, where charters are handed out like Halloween candy, charter schools fail quite often.) On the other side, the powerful NEA continues to insist that teachers be paid based on years of service, despite overwhelming evidence that those days are over, now that everyone else from President Obama on down insists that student learning matters more than a teacher's experience.

But what's most striking about this bitter battle is its irrelevance. The adults in charge are fighting the last war, and it doesn't really matter who wins to the millions of young people now being denied on a daily basis the learning opportunities that modern technology affords.

Our young people should be learning how to deal with the flood of information that surrounds them. They need guidance separating wheat from chaff. They need help formulating questions, and they need to develop the habit of seeking answers, not regurgitating them. They should be going to schools where they are expected and encouraged to discover, build, and cooperate.

Instead, most of them endure what I call "regurgitation education" and are stuck in institutions that expect them to memorize the periodic table, the names of 50 state capitals, and the major rivers of the United States.

SO WHAT'S TO BE DONE?

My premise is simple: To solve public education's problem, the first step is to give it a name. Is it a *Better People* problem, or is the job of teaching the core issue?

Deep down many of us just know that great teachers are the key. We know it because of a teacher in fourth grade who encouraged us to keep on drawing. Or a seventh-grade social studies teacher who brought history to life and convinced us that politics could be honorable. Or the homeroom teacher in high school who always took time to listen but also insisted that we do our best. Because of a special teacher or two, when we hear about education's problems, we know deep down that all would be well if today's schools only had more great teachers like those.

On the other hand, suppose you are one of the millions who gave up on teaching, frustrated by its pettiness and daily humiliations. You might still be in front of a classroom if conditions had been different. And so you know in your heart that the root of education's problem is the job and its lousy working conditions.

That's the dilemma, and the ongoing battle: Are mediocre teachers the heart of education's problems? Or is it the job itself, with its low pay and even lower prestige? Those two very different analyses of education's problem are competing for domination, and whoever gets to define the problem is likely to control education policies for many years.

There's an inescapable irony here. Just as a *Better Job* has been narrowly defined by numbers (more money, fewer students), *Better People* also are defined by numbers. Although adjectives like *dedicated, hard working,* and *uncomplaining* are thrown around freely in conversation, the bottom line is test scores. That's what *Better People* do in the classroom—they move the needle.

And therein lies a flaw in the *Better People* approach, because even if they do move the needle, the vast majority of teachers from Teach for America are unlikely to stick around beyond their 2-year commitment.

Suppose for the sake of argument that 20% of our teachers are no longer willing or able to do the job. That's 400,000 teachers who ought to be removed and replaced, if efforts to retrain them fail. But if they are replaced by men and women who themselves depart after 2 or perhaps 3 years, the system remains a revolving door, with one group of *Better People* replacing another. At the end of the day, we are no better off.

CONCLUSIONS

To me, a more sensible path entails redefining *Better Job*, but that won't be easy. Narrow and restrictive union contracts must be negotiated away or overturned, so that a principal will not have to bargain with teachers about coming into their classrooms, for example. The same school boards that agreed to idiotic and restrictive contracts favoring teachers now must have the courage to say no. Both boards and unions need to somehow put the interests of children first.

Unions here have to become what their counterparts are in Finland and other places where schools outperform ours: They must become professional unions, not trade unions. In May 2011 Weingarten and then-NEA Executive Director John Wilson publicly agreed that they could envision writing a model professional contract, one that would be less than 20 pages long (as opposed to many current contracts that run hundreds of pages). I proposed the same change, incidentally, at a colloquium sponsored by the National Center for Education and the Economy, and that group's leader, Marc Tucker, subsequently enlisted the services of two former U.S. Secretaries of Labor, Ray Marshall and William Brock, to work on the effort. That's promising, so stay tuned.

Teaching will be a *Better Job* when:

1. Principals have authority over hiring their staff but are savvy about bringing trusted veteran teachers into the process.
2. Teacher evaluations of students count at least as much as the score on a one-time standardized test.
3. Employment contracts are not for life and employee evaluations are fair and thorough, with all due process rights respected.
4. Everyone's pay depends in part on how students perform academically. However, merit bonuses must go to the school's entire staff, so that the art, music, and physical education teachers and even the school secretary have a vested interest in success. There's no need to add standardized testing in more subjects. Instead, create conditions that encourage physical education teachers, for example, to build math into their classes. (Don't just throw the football, but graph the results for distance and accuracy.)
5. We recognize that the world has changed and the job of a teacher is to help young people learn to ask good questions, because good questions invariably lead to more questions. With the flood of information around them, young people need help separating wheat from chaff. And it's no longer the teacher's job to tell them the difference, but to give them the skills to inquire, to dig deeper.

And when teaching becomes the *Better Job* as described above, the brain drain will no longer be a problem—and we may discover that many teachers now in the classroom have been *Better People* themselves all along.

CHAPTER 9

Waiting for "Superman": A Response

Ben Levin

Although *Waiting for "Superman"* is a distinctly American production, it got quite a bit of attention in Canada as well, perhaps in part because of its launch at the Toronto International Film Festival in September 2010. This attention is symptomatic of the attention Canada gives to education developments in the United States, even though public education in Canada is very different from U.S. public education in many respects.

In this chapter I want to make two points. The first is how odd the ideas and perspectives in *Waiting for "Superman"* appear outside the United States, where the whole education debate is quite different. The second point is that *Waiting for "Superman"* does not actually talk about teaching and learning so its ideas and analysis cannot really be the basis for a sound strategy for systemic improvement.

A movie is, of course, a simplification, and usually one designed to appeal more to our emotions than to our intellect (although the best films do both). *Waiting for "Superman"* is very much in the emotional appeal category, with its heartwrenching shots of young people who are clearly not being well served by schools, and the very long (indeed, I would say interminable) final section in which kids and parents wait for the lottery results. It is also planted firmly in the world of American individualism, only occasionally mentioning that for every child who is successful in a lottery, another one is not. The film is all about individual students and their families, even though, as it suggests, the real issue is quality across the entire system. In that regard, the central emotional element of the film—rooting for those five young people to "win"—is entirely inconsistent with its central intellectual point, which is that the system as a whole is not adequately serving large numbers of young people, and particularly those from poor and minority backgrounds. (And was it an accident that the only White student in the group was the only one to succeed in the lottery at the end of the film?)

LEARNING FROM OTHER COUNTRIES

Let's consider how the ideas in *Waiting for "Superman"* relate to education issues and debates in many other parts of the world. In March 2011, Secretary of Education Arne Duncan convened, in New York, a meeting of ministers of education and teacher leaders from 15 countries to discuss "the future of the teaching profession," which I had the opportunity to attend as one of four "rapporteurs." The other countries included Japan, Singapore, China, England, the Netherlands, Finland, Poland, and Canada, among others. One of the main takeaways from that conversation was that the United States is on a different path to education improvement than virtually every other country at the meeting.[1] Dominant ideas in the United States today focus on charter schools, competition, testing with potentially serious results for both students and schools, alternative certification, merit pay for teachers, and firing bad teachers.

In virtually every other country at the meeting, almost all of which have higher levels of performance than the United States, the dominant ideas are very different.[2] They center on helping teachers and principals improve their work, building a feeling of common purpose among all partners, and creating a positive environment that focuses on continuous improvement and high morale. Other countries are not less committed to better outcomes; indeed, judging by results, they are more committed. They have chosen different routes to get there and, again judging by results, routes that seem more effective. They have concluded that you cannot build a great school system by beating up on the people who work in it. They have concluded that motivation is a less central problem than are skills, so that simply urging people to do better, or punishing those who do not, is not going to be a workable solution. Instead, these systems focus on supporting educators in improving their skills, reasoning that the more skilled people are, the more motivated they are to use those skills.

Virtually every international analysis confirms the need to focus on building capacity in the system for improvement. The OECD studies on teachers,[3] which were presented at the New York meeting by Andreas Schleicher, stressed the importance not just of recruiting good people into teaching, but even more of developing and supporting teachers once they enter the profession. The recent McKinsey report on good school systems also has the same message.[4]

It is worth noting, too, how different the dominant U.S. policy discourse on education is from the country's approach to most other areas of activity. The United States does not close hospitals with poor health results. It does not punish doctors with lower effectiveness in treating patients. Performance is related to rewards only through public reputation, which often is based on rumor or advertising. There is no relationship at all between corporate CEOs' record of profit and their compensation,[5] and in many cases CEOs who do badly are bought off with huge payments, something nobody has yet suggested for teachers or even superintendents. The country does not fire soldiers who cannot do the work being asked of them. Indeed, the U.S. military is a prime example of an organization that tries never to quit on its people and assumes that many of them, even if they start with relatively low levels of education, can master complex technical and leadership skills given enough high-quality training and support.

Similarly, there is no other profession in the United States where it is proposed that people be paid based on the outcomes of their clients. Many professionals are paid based on volume, and this may depend on reputation, but they are not paid based on any measured outcomes. Indeed, other than salespeople, hardly anyone in the entire labor force is paid based on a measured outcome.[6] These points, of course, never appear in *Waiting for "Superman."*

Moreover, in most parts of the world, education is seen as being embedded in the larger society; the success of schools is deeply affected by how the society addresses issues such as health, housing, wages, and employment. In a compelling analysis of international and U.S. data, Wilkinson and Pickett show how virtually all desirable social outcomes are connected to the degree of inequality inside societies.[7] Across countries, those with less income inequality have consistently better outcomes, whether in education, health, crime, or other areas. The same relationship holds true, and just as strongly, among U.S. states. Yes, what schools do still matters. I am not suggesting that everything depends on social policy rather than on education. But it is equally unreasonable to argue that schools alone can overcome all the deleterious effects of highly unequal societies. And the United States is a society that tolerates very high levels of inequality in virtually every sphere, seeing them as the inevitable price of individual freedom. Other countries do not share that belief.

In this light, the main themes in *Waiting for "Superman"* seem, to many people around the world, quite incongruous and disconnected from what really needs to be done to provide excellent public education for all young people. High-quality systems do not depend on lotteries; they strive to reduce the impact of socioeconomic status on school outcomes. At the same time, no country is entirely successful in doing so; social origins continue to be powerful influences on education and life outcomes everywhere in the world, but they are much more powerful in some places—such as the United States—than in others.

There are, however, some grounds for hope. Although the United States continues—as has been characteristic of dominant powers throughout history—to believe strongly in its own exceptionalism and moral superiority, there are increasing signs of attention in the United States to what is happening in education in other countries. The analyses mentioned earlier, and the very fact of the New York meeting (and the apparent intention to hold another one in 2012), show an interest in learning from other countries that previously has not been evident. While there are many criticisms of international assessments such as PISA or TIMSS, one must be happy that they have provided some solid evidence that public education in the United States is not the most successful in the world, and that the United States can learn from looking at other countries' practices, policies, and experiences. The province of Ontario, where I live and work, has always received many delegations of visitors, but in the past few years, for the first time, a number of U.S. groups have come to look at our education system and its achievements.

None of this is to suggest that policies can be plunked from one country into another with much hope of success. Just as efforts to export U.S. policies of competition, assessment, and accountability have been resisted in many parts of the world and had little positive impact in other places, so it would not make sense to suggest that the United States could or should have an education system that resembles that of Singapore. But at its best, the international exchange helps people in each setting see their own world from outside, with a little more objectivity, and helps us all think about how we could improve our own situation, taking into account all its historical and institutional individuality. Any serious attempt to do that work in the United States would conclude that the current dominant policy approaches have little hope of leading to real, widespread, and lasting improvement.

WHAT COUNTS: GOOD TEACHING AND LEARNING

This leads to the second major problem with *Waiting for "Superman"* that I want to raise, which is that there is virtually no discussion in it of what counts as good teaching and learning, or of how we can have more of it in our schools. The movie introduces us to Geoffrey Canada as an example of vision in education—which he undoubtedly is. But what is it that happens in his schools in order to get those better results from students? Surely it can't simply be a matter of passion and caring; if that were all it took, then all those who wanted to be good at something, would be. But as we know, being good at anything is a matter of much more than desire. Skills are developed through practice and coaching, and results come from systematic efforts, not just through motivation and exhortation. This is undoubtedly one reason the movie notes that charter schools do not have better success records on average than public schools—because either they do not have a solid theory of how to produce better outcomes, or their theory is not accurate, or they do not know how to put that theory into action reliably on almost all occasions.

Teaching well is complex and difficult. Good teachers have to have a deep knowledge of their subject matter, a deep understanding of how to teach that material, and a deep knowledge of their students, individually and collectively. Sometimes knowing one's subject really well makes it harder to teach it well, as one has less empathy for those who cannot grasp it readily. That is why just being a subject expert is not nearly enough to be a good teacher, just as being the best player does not make one the best coach, or being the best musician does not make one the best orchestra leader. An hour or two in many university classrooms should convince anyone that expertise and teaching skill are not the same thing. Surely it would be good to have more people in teaching with a deep knowledge of mathematics or science or history, but that alone—even if it were possible to do, which is by no means obvious—would not make those people good teachers.

It seems essential, then, that an effort to improve schooling across an entire system or country would have to pay attention to improving the skills and practices of large numbers of teachers—of whom there are some 3 million in U.S. public schools. When put this way, the task is clearly daunting. That may be one reason for efforts to create programmatic models, or what once were called "teacher-proof" methods. However, those did not work well either—because teaching cannot be reduced to a set of prescribed technical activities. It requires, like any other skilled activity, ongoing decisions by practitioners as to how to apply their knowledge to particular situations. Classrooms being complex places with many students, each of whom is, at least in some ways, different from all the others, it seems unlikely that a scripted approach can be successful.

On the other hand, to say that one cannot script teaching, does not take us to the opposite position—that each classroom is unique and that there are no common practices or guidelines that should be used consistently, if not universally. As our knowledge of teaching and learning improves, we have more grounds for encouraging practices with a good base of evidence. Examples would include the use of formative assessment, the value of supporting students' first language, the importance of balanced literacy, and many others.[8] Ironically, while education systems have a long history of imposing untested practices on teachers, the capacity to build on and use reasonably well-validated knowledge is largely absent. There is no educational equivalent to the idea of clinical guidelines such as exist (albeit quite imperfectly) in medicine, or of practice guidelines in many other professions.

Moreover, teaching is a social activity. Although one often hears about teachers doing whatever they choose "after they shut the classroom door," in fact teaching practice is social. It is quite hard to be the only teacher in a school with a particular method or approach. New teachers typically are socialized rapidly into the norms of their schools, which would not be the case if teaching were as individual and isolated as is often claimed (and which is why, incidentally, simply focusing on initial teacher education is not a good way to generate improved schooling).

The social nature of teaching and schooling means that improvement is not just a matter of what individual teachers do. The larger context in which they work, whether school, district, or state, also matters. The curriculum framework, the approach to assessment, the culture of the school, the collegiality among staff, the degree to which principals support ongoing teacher learning—all these features have an important impact on how teachers work and what students experience. Those relationships are not one-way, which is why just changing policies on these matters rarely produces the desired results. But an approach to school improvement also has to take into account system-level effects on teaching and on students.

None of this complexity appears in *Waiting for "Superman,"* either in relation to the nature and importance of teaching, or in relation to the need for coherent and aligned policy and supports for good teaching. We learn nothing at all about effective schools or teachers in terms of the specific practices they use. Success is portrayed as a matter of getting the right teachers— whatever that means—and freeing them from the dead hand of large organizations. But without a clearly articulated theory of good teaching and learning, it is hard to see how any proposals are going to be successful in helping students, and we have many years of failed efforts to reinforce that point, if we care to pay attention.

Systems that have shown significant improvement have done so through a thoughtful combination of policy and support for good practice. Successful systems around the world, and even within the United States, do not rely on a small set of nostrums, as suggested by *Waiting for "Superman."* They rightly understand schooling as a complex process in which many things matter and require attention. Countries such as Singapore, Korea, and Finland have shown dramatic improvements in outcomes over a generation. Ontario has shown large improvements in student outcomes and in teacher morale in the past 8 years.[9] These have not come from any of the ideas in *Waiting for "Superman"*—not from competition, not from union-bashing, not from decentralization, and not from stronger accountability. They have come from using what we know about improving any large system—a focus on a few clear goals, constant support for people to improve their skills, strengthening teamwork and organizational alignment, effective use of data to guide further improvement, and relentless attention to the central task. The unwillingness of so many U.S. education policy advocates to acknowledge this is hard to fathom.

A 90-minute movie is a limited vehicle for understanding any complex social phenomenon. It is unfair to expect *Waiting for "Superman"* or any similar movie to say all that needs to be said. It is fair, however, to expect that a movie will not take people down a blind alley, and on that test, it is hard to be positive about *Waiting for "Superman."*

NOTES

1. Asia Society, *Improving Teacher Quality Around the World: The International Summit on the Teaching Profession* (New York: Asia Society, 2011).

2. OECD, *Strong Performers and Successful Reformers* (Paris: OECD, 2011).

3. OECD, *Building a High-Quality Teaching Profession: Lessons from Around the World.* Paper prepared for the international Summit on the Future of the Teaching Profession (Paris: OECD, 2011).

4. M. Mourshed, C. Chijioke, and M. Barber, *How the World's Most Improved School Systems Keep Getting Better* (New York: McKinsey & Co., 2010).

5. J. Pfeffer and R. Sutton, *Hard Facts, Dangerous Half-Truths and Total Nonsense: Profiting from Evidence-Based Management* (Boston: Harvard Business School Press, 2006).

6. S. Adams and J. Heywood, "Performance Pay in the U S Private Sector: Concepts, Measurement, and Trends," in *Teachers, Performance Pay, and Accountability: What Education Should Learn from Other Sectors,* eds. S. Adams, J. Heywood, and R. Rothstein (Washington, DC: Economic Policy Institute, 2009), 11–64.

7. R. Wilkinson and K. Pickett, *The Spirit Level: Why Equality Is Better for Everyone.* (London: Penguin Books, 2009).

8. J. Hattie, *Visible Learning: A Synthesis of Over 800 Meta-Analyses Relating to Achievement* (United Kingdom: Routledge, 2009), 1–375.

9. B. Levin, *How to Change 5000 Schools* (Cambridge, MA: Harvard Education Press, 2008).

About the Contributors

Milton Chen is senior fellow and executive director emeritus at The George Lucas Educational Foundation. His career has spanned 4 decades at the intersection of media, technology, and learning as founding director of the KQED Center for Education (PBS) and director of research at Sesame Workshop. Dr. Chen has taught at the Harvard Graduate School of Education and been a Fulbright New Century Scholar at the University of Edinburgh. He chairs the advisory council for the Fred Rogers Center for Early Learning and Children's Media at St. Vincent College and is a member of the National Park System advisory board. He serves on the board of directors of ConnectEd: The California Center for College and Career and the San Francisco School Alliance. His work has been honored by the Corporation for Public Broadcasting's Fred Rogers Award, Sesame Workshop's Elmo Award, the Association of Educational Service Agencies, the Congressional Black Caucus, and two science centers, the Exploratorium and the Lawrence Hall of Science.

Linda Darling-Hammond is Charles E. Ducommun Professor of Education at Stanford University where she has launched the Stanford Educational Leadership Institute and the School Redesign Network. She also has served as faculty sponsor for the Stanford Teacher Education Program. She is a former president of the American Educational Research Association and member of the National Academy of Education. Her research, teaching, and policy work focus on issues of school restructuring, teacher quality, and educational equity. From 1994–2001, she served as executive director of the National Commission on Teaching and America's Future, a blue-ribbon panel whose 1996 report, "What Matters Most: Teaching for America's Future," led to sweeping policy changes affecting teaching and teacher education. In 2006, this report was named one of the most influential affecting U.S. education, and Darling-Hammond was named one of the nation's ten most influential people affecting educational policy over the past decade. Among Darling-Hammond's more than 300 publications are *Preparing Teachers for a Changing World: What Teachers Should Learn and Be Able to Do* (with John Bransford, for the National Academy of Education, winner of the Pomeroy Award from AACTE), *Teaching as the Learning Profession: A Handbook of Policy and Practice* (Jossey-Bass, 1999; co-edited with Gary Sykes), which received the National Staff Development Council's Outstanding Book Award for 2000; and *The Right to Learn: A Blueprint for Schools That Work*, recipient of the American Educational Research Association's Outstanding Book Award for 1998.

Daniel A. Domenech has served as executive director of the American Association of School Administrators since July 2008. Domenech has more than 36 years of experience in public education, 27 of those years as a school superintendent. Prior to joining AASA, Domenech served as senior vice president for National Urban Markets with McGraw-Hill Education. In this role, he was responsible for building strong relationships with large school districts nationwide. Prior to his position at McGraw-Hill, Domenech served for 7 years as superintendent of the Fairfax County, Virginia Public Schools, the 12th largest school system in the nation with 168,000 students. In addition, Domenech has served on the U.S. Department of Education's National Assessment Governing Board, on the advisory board for the Department of Defense schools, and on the board of directors of the Association for the Advancement of International Education. He currently serves on the Board of Overseers for the Baldrige Award and on the boards of the Institute for Educational Leadership, the National Board for Professional Teaching Standards, and the Education Policy Institute, and is chair for Communities in Schools of Virginia.

Ben Levin is a professor and Canada Research Chair in Education Leadership and Policy at the Ontario Institute for Studies in Education, University of Toronto. His career has been about evenly divided between academia and the senior civil service. He has just completed a second short stint as Deputy Minister (chief civil servant) for Education for the Province of Ontario (he also served in that role from 2004–2007). From 1999 through 2002, he was Deputy Minister of Advanced Education and Deputy Minister of Education, Training and Youth for the Province of Manitoba. Dr. Levin has worked with private research organizations, school districts, provincial governments, and national and international agencies, as well as building an academic and research career. He has published five books, most recently, *How to Change 5000 Schools*, and more than 200 articles on education. His current interests are large-scale change, poverty and inequity, and finding better ways to connect research to policy and practice in education.

Arthur Levine is president of the Woodrow Wilson National Fellowship Foundation and president emeritus of Teachers College, Columbia University. He previously served as chair of the higher education program, chair of the Institute for Educational Management, and senior lecturer at the Harvard Graduate School of Education. Dr. Levine is the author or co-author of numerous books, articles, and reviews on American education, including a series of noted reports for the Education Schools Project on the preparation of school leaders, teachers, and education researchers. Much of his research and writing in recent years has focused on increasing access to higher education and improving equity in schools. He has received numerous honors, including a Guggenheim Fellowship and a Carnegie Fellowship, as well as the American Council on Education's Book of the Year award, and he is a Fellow of the American Academy of Arts and Sciences.

Ann Lieberman is an emeritus professor from Teachers College, Columbia University, and was a senior scholar at the Carnegie Foundation for the Advancement of Teaching. She is now a senior scholar at Stanford University. Her recent books include *Teachers in Professional Communities: Improving Teaching and Learning* (with Lynne Miller) and *How Teachers Learn to Lead* (with Linda Friedrich). Her unique contribution has been the ability to go between school and university, embracing the dualities that plague the field—theory/practice; process/content; intellectual/social-emotional learning; policy/practice—thereby helping to build a more comprehensive understanding of teachers and schools and what it will take to involve them in deepening their work. In doing this, she has fashioned a way to be both a scholar and an activist, a practitioner and a theoretician.

John Merrow is a broadcast journalist who has reported on education issues for more than 3 decades. He serves as the education correspondent for the PBS *NewsHour* program. Additionally, he is currently the executive producer, host, and president of Learning Matters, Inc., a not-for-profit corporation that creates television, radio, and online segments and documentaries, focusing primarily on education. Merrow is a graduate from the Harvard Graduate School of Education, with a doctorate in education and social policy. He began his career as an education reporter in 1974 and later produced a seven-part television series for PBS along the same lines, entitled *Your Children, Our Children.* This program received an Emmy nomination in 1984. In 1998, he created Listen Up!, a project that trains disadvantaged youth and their teachers in broadcast production skills and techniques. He received the George Foster Peabody Award in 2001 for "School Sleuth: The Case of an Excellent School" and won a second Peabody Award for Listen Up!'s production, "Beyond Borders," in 2006. In 2005 and 2007, Learning Matters's programming received Emmy nominations. Merrow is also author of the book *Choosing Excellence* (2001) and co-editor (with Richard Hersh) of *Declining by Degrees* (2005). Merrow is a trustee of Teachers College, Columbia University, and serves on the board of the Education Writers Association.

Diane Ravitch is research professor of education at New York University and a historian of education. In addition, she is a nonresident senior fellow at the Brookings Institution in Washington, DC. From 1991 to 1993, she was Assistant Secretary of Education and Counselor to Secretary of Education Lamar Alexander in the administration of President George H. W. Bush. She was responsible for the Office of Educational Research and Improvement in the U.S. Department of Education. From 1997 to 2004, she was a member of the National Assessment Governing Board, which oversees the National Assessment of Educational Progress, the federal testing program. She was appointed by the Clinton administration's Secretary of Education Richard Riley in 1997 and reappointed by him in 2001. From 1995 until 2005, she held the Brown Chair in Education Studies at the Brookings Institution and edited *Brookings Papers on Education Policy.* Before entering government service, she was Adjunct Professor of History and Education at Teachers College, Columbia University.

Peter Smith is Senior Vice President of Academic Strategies and Development for Kaplan Higher Education. He is the former assistant director general of education at UNESCO and served as the founding president of California

State University at Monterey Bay (CSUMB). Smith led a successful effort to implement Vermont's community college system, which included the design of its operating, administrative, academic, and assessment systems, and served as its first president. He served as Vermont's lieutenant governor from 1982 to 1986 and in 1989 was elected as a representative from Vermont to the U.S. House of Representatives. Dr. Smith is the author of the critically acclaimed *The Quiet Crisis: How Higher Education Is Failing America.*

Watson Scott Swail is president and chief executive officer of the Educational Policy Institute, a nonprofit, nongovernmental organization dedicated to policy-based research on educational opportunity for all students. Widely respected in the area of college opportunity research, Dr. Swail has published extensively in national journals and publications. Recent publications include "Latino Students and the Educational Pipeline," "The Affordability of Higher Education," and "Higher Education and the New Demographics." He has been published in *Phi Delta Kappan, Change,* and the *Chronicle of Higher Education.* Dr. Swail has served on a number of national advisory committees, including technical review panels for the major U.S. longitudinal and cross-sectional surveys sponsored by the U.S. Department of Education's National Center for Education Statistics. In addition, he recently has conducted projects for the Canada Millennium Scholarship Program related to postsecondary access in Canada. Prior to establishing EPI, Dr. Swail served as the founding director of the Pell Institute and vice president of the Council for Opportunity in Education in Washington, DC. He previously served as senior policy analyst with SRI International and associate director for policy analysis with the College Board.

Index